T0372648

Life without God

In this book, Rik Peels explores atheism from a new perspective that aims to go beyond the highly polarized debate about arguments for and against God's existence. Since our beliefs about the most important things in life are not usually based on arguments, we should look beyond atheistic arguments and explore what truly motivates the atheist. Are there certain ideals or experiences that explain the turn to atheism? Could atheism be the default position for us, not requiring any arguments whatsoever? And what about the often-discussed arguments against belief in God – is there something that religious and nonreligious people alike can learn from them? This book explores how a novel understanding of atheism is possible – and how it effectively moves the God debate further. Believers and nonbelievers can learn much from Peels's assessment of arguments for and against atheism.

RIK PEELS is Associate Professor of Philosophy and Theology & Religion at the Vrije Universiteit Amsterdam. He is the author of *Ignorance: A Philosophical Study* (Oxford University Press, 2023) and *Responsible Belief: A Theory in Ethics and Epistemology* (Oxford University Press, 2017). He leads an international project on the epistemology and ethics of extreme beliefs.

Vrije Universiteit Amsterdam

Life without God
An Outsider's Look at Atheism

CAMBRIDGE
UNIVERSITY PRESS

Shaftesbury Road, Cambridge CB2 8EA, United Kingdom

One Liberty Plaza, 20th Floor, New York, NY 10006, USA

477 Williamstown Road, Port Melbourne, VIC 3207, Australia

314–321, 3rd Floor, Plot 3, Splendor Forum, Jasola District Centre,
New Delhi – 110025, India

103 Penang Road, #05–06/07, Visioncrest Commercial, Singapore 238467

Cambridge University Press is part of Cambridge University Press & Assessment,
a department of the University of Cambridge.

We share the University's mission to contribute to society through the pursuit of
education, learning and research at the highest international levels of excellence.

www.cambridge.org
Information on this title: www.cambridge.org/9781009297820

DOI: 10.1017/9781009297790

© Cambridge University Press & Assessment 2023

First published 2023

A catalogue record for this publication is available from the British Library.

*A Cataloging-in-Publication data record for this book is available from the Library
of Congress.*

ISBN 978-1-009-29782-0 Hardback
ISBN 978-1-009-29777-6 Paperback

To all those who sincerely seek truth.

Contents

Acknowledgments   *page* viii

1   A New Approach to Atheism   1

2   Motivations for Atheism   17

3   Atheistic Frameworks   50

4   The Presumption of Atheism   89

5   Atheistic Arguments and Faith   117

6   Atheistic Arguments and God   145

7   Life after Atheism   174

Selected Bibliography   191
Index   195

Acknowledgments

For sharp and helpful comments on various parts of the manuscript or ideas expressed in it, I'd like to thank Valentin Arts, Max Baker-Hytch, Henk Bakker, Jan Boersema, Michiel Bouman, Kelly James Clark, Bart Cusveller, Leon de Bruin, Andries de Jong, Jeroen de Ridder, Ninya den Haan, Elaine Howard Ecklund, Coos Engelsma, Jacques Esselink, René Fransen, Harmen Ghijsen, Gerrit Glas, Scott Gustafson, Christian Hofreiter, Jeroen Hopster, Simon Howard, Dan Howard-Snyder, Wilfred Jacobs, Judith Janssen, Maarten Kater, Bart Klink, Erkki Vesa Rope Kojonen, Brian Leftow, Ard Louis, Tim Mawson, Boaz Miller, Fred Muller, Chris Oldfield, Stefan Paas, my father Eric Peels, Herman Philipse, Alvin Plantinga, Paul Rezkalla, Emanuel Rutten, Ewoud Schmidt, Koert van Bekkum, Gijsbert van den Brink, Hans Van Eyghen, Niels van Miltenburg, Anne van Mulligen, René van Woudenberg, Joeri Witteveen, Laura Rogers Ziesel, and two anonymous referees for Cambridge University Press.

I warmly thank my students in two classes at the Vrije Universiteit Amsterdam: Secular Worldviews in January 2020 and Systematic Theology in September 2021. I'd also like to thank the audiences at a meeting of the Joseph Butler Society at Oriel College in Oxford (2012), at the European Leadership Forum in Wisła in Poland (2014), at the Cambridge Scholars Network meeting in Moggerhanger Park in the United Kingdom (2018), at the Developing a Christian Mind Club at my friends Ard and Mary Louis's home in Oxford (2019), and at the international conference on rationality, theism, and atheism in Teheran in Iran (2021).

I am grateful to Beatrice Rehl, Thirumangai Thamizhmani, Sarah Wales-McGrath, and their colleagues at Cambridge University Press: their enthusiasm and constructive support have made for an encouraging and swift process in getting this book published. Mathanja Berger did a fantastic job in making the manuscript ready for the publisher, providing insightful philosophical and theological comments along the way as well. I thank the Templeton World Charity Foundation, whose support made the publication of this book possible. The opinions expressed in this publication are mine and do not necessarily reflect the views of the Templeton World Charity Foundation. Work on this book was also made possible by my project Extreme Beliefs: The Epistemology and Ethics of Fundamentalism, which has received funding from the European Research Council (ERC) under the European Union's Horizon 2020 research and innovation program (grant agreement no. 851613) and from the Vrije Universiteit Amsterdam. Above all, I thank my wonderful wife, Marjolijn Peels-de Waal, for the many inspiring conversations we've had on the issues explored in this book.

1 | A New Approach to Atheism

Arguing and Persuading

One night, I was watching a debate between American philosopher William Lane Craig and British biologist Lewis Wolpert in Central Hall Westminster. They debated with each other on the question "Is God an illusion?" Craig devoted his introductory speech to no fewer than five arguments for God's existence, which he laid out carefully, premise by premise, showing how the conclusion should follow deductively from the premises. When Wolpert came to the stage, he did something completely different. Here are some crucial quotes from his 15-minute opening speech:

> It's quite a complex issue. And let me try to explain to you why.... I'm not against people being religious. I believe it helps you a great deal.... So, I'm not against people having a belief in God. I do believe that their belief is false.... Beliefs are like possessions, and I ask you: When did you really last give up a basic belief or your partner or your parent or your child? It's very hard to do so.... Now, if you believe that [God deliberately designed and created the universe and human beings] (and many of you do believe that), you feel better. And that, I regret to tell you, is why you believe in it. And that really is the origin of religion.... Now, the problem about believing in God is looking for evidence. I regret to tell you ... there is zero evidence for the existence of God. I'm terribly sorry, there just isn't.... Let me try to explain to you – you won't like it one bit – as to why you actually believe in God. First of all, it makes you

feel better; you have someone to pray to…. And so, I'm sorry to tell you – you won't like it, it's not attractive – the origin of religion comes from toolmaking…. And prayer is very comforting, even though it may not lead anywhere…. I'm sorry to tell you, you and all human beings have quite a strong set of mystical circuits in your brain, and it comes, I would want to argue, from the fact that those people who believed in religion and mysticism survived better in our ancestors than those who did not.[1]

I was stunned. How could one take a position in a debate and then not come up with any rigorous arguments for it? Just to be clear: I myself have debated several atheists who did come up with various serious arguments. However, why was Wolpert not doing that? And how come there was nonetheless something appealing, something persuasive, about what he said? How come the audience seemed to like and in fact cheered what he said?

I've rewatched that opening speech time and again. As I see it now, Wolpert presents a couple of somewhat sketchy arguments against God's existence and against belief in God. Any student who has taken an introductory course in elementary argumentation theory will easily dispel these arguments. The force of what Wolpert says is not in the arguments but in the implicit messages that can be heard between the lines. I think he conveys at least three such messages:

- The issue is complex and challenging, but I have a firm grip on it. I've been there, don't worry. I'll walk you through it; let's go!
- If you want to be happy, it helps to be religious. However, if, like me, you value truth more than your own happiness, then follow me. I'm a great scientist, and I know what science says about religion. Do you dare to face the truth?

---

[1] The full video is available at www.ReasonableFaith.org. It is also available on YouTube: www.youtube.com/watch?v=n2wh179k0so.

- I am a good-natured and sympathetic guy. After all, I'm very sorry to tell you the harsh truth. So, don't worry about rejecting the existence of God. You can be an atheist and still lead a valuable, moral, and fulfilling life.

Could it be that in the countless books, articles, blogs, public debates, and videos on atheism, we have been missing something? And when I say *we*, I mean *all* of us: atheists, agnostics, and religious believers alike. Much attention has been paid to whether or not the arguments for and against God's existence are convincing. Atheists have delved into the intuitions, experiences, psychological factors, and many other elements that supposedly explain why people believe in God. But what motivates atheism? What is life without God like? Are atheists really primarily motivated by arguments against belief in God, or is the attraction of life without God to be found in something else?

Atheism has received plenty of public attention, especially since the rise of *New Atheism*. This new branch of atheism is a twenty-first-century phenomenon and has become widely known by the bestsellers and public talks of four figures in particular: Richard Dawkins, Daniel Dennett, Christopher Hitchens, and Sam Harris. Critics of the movement have referred to them as the "four horsemen of atheism," an allusion to the apocalyptic appearance of four horses and their riders in Revelation 6, who symbolize such things as famine and death. Understandably, New Atheists themselves generally prefer slightly different labels, such as "the Brights." New Atheists have debated their opponents on the allegedly immoral doctrines and abject practices of several religions, the soundness of various arguments for God's existence, the presumed dangers of atheism, and the relation between science and religion. This New Atheism has been vigorously criticized not only by religious believers, like Alister McGrath and John Lennox, but equally by other contemporary atheists, like John Gray.[2]

---

[2] See, respectively, Alister McGrath, *The Twilight of Atheism: The Rise and Fall of Disbelief in the Modern World* (London: Rider, 2004); John Lennox, *Gunning for*

To study atheism itself rather than assess the soundness of various atheistic arguments is merely to catch up with what atheists have been doing regarding religion. It is quite common among atheists to psychologically explain religion away. Says A. C. Grayling:

> The major reason for the continuance of religious belief in a world which might otherwise have long moved beyond it, is indoctrination of children before they reach the age of reason, together with all or some combination of social pressure to conform, social reinforcement of religious institutions and traditions, emotion, and (it has to be said) ignorance – of science, of psychology, of history in general, and of the history and actual doctrines of religions themselves.[3]

This is, of course, not only polemical and offensive but also particularly ill-informed. Anyone working in the field of the cognitive science of religion – the scientific discipline that provides naturalistic explanations for belief in God and religious experience – will tell you that indoctrination can't do the job, not even in combination with other social phenomena like pressure and reinforcement. But the more important point is this: atheists have paid plenty of attention to what motivates religious believers. Rather than being obsessed with theistic arguments, they have rightly addressed every aspect of a religious worldview. Time has come for atheism to be explored in a similar way.

In this book, the aim is to better understand but also fairly evaluate atheism. Why is it so attractive to many nowadays – what motivates the atheist? Apart from the affective appeal, are there particular cognitive frameworks or ways of thinking that are conducive to atheism? Can atheism perhaps be the default position? And putting the issue of the soundness of atheistic arguments aside, what can

---

God: A Critique of the New Atheism (Oxford: Lion, 2011); and John Gray, *Seven Types of Atheism* (London: Penguin Books, 2018).

[3] A. C. Grayling, *The God Argument: The Case against Religion and for Humanism* (London: Bloomsbury, 2013), 13.

we learn from them? Do these arguments perhaps contain insights for everyone, atheists and religious believers included? I believe the debate so far has been somewhat obsessed with whether arguments for and against God's existence are convincing. We've overlooked important and fascinating issues. Here, we'll see whether we can set things straight.

What Is Atheism?

There are two crucially different ways to define *atheism*. First, atheism can be the lack of belief in any kind of god.[4] Some call this *negative theism*. An example of this is how John Gray characterizes what it is to be an atheist: "An atheist is anyone with no use for the idea of a divine mind that has fashioned the world."[5] If one has no use for the idea of a divine mind, one might simply suspend judgment on whether there is such a divine mind. A stronger position is atheism as the belief or conviction that there are no gods.[6] Some call this *positive atheism*.[7]

When I talk about atheism, I have the stronger version in mind. This is because most vocal atheists nowadays are actually positive atheists. Moreover, there is already another word for the weaker position, namely, *agnosticism*. An agnostic doesn't know whether there is a God; there may well be and there may well not be. Some agnostics even claim that we cannot possibly know whether or not

---

[4] E.g., Stephen Bullivant, "Defining 'Atheism,'" in *The Oxford Handbook of Atheism*, ed. Stephen Bullivant and Michael Ruse (Oxford: Oxford University Press, 2013), 11–21; Michael Martin, *Atheism: A Philosophical Justification* (Philadelphia: Temple University Press, 1990).

[5] See Gray, *Seven Types of Atheism*, 2. See also Bullivant, "Defining 'Atheism,'" 14.

[6] Julian Baggini, *Atheism: A Very Short Introduction* (Oxford: Oxford University Press, 2003), 3; Paul Cliteur, "The Definition of Atheism," *Journal of Religion and Society* 11 (2009): 1–23; McGrath, *The Twilight of Atheism*, 175.

[7] E.g., Bullivant, "Defining 'Atheism,'" 14.

there is a God. A famous example of an agnostic is Charles Darwin's bulldog – his advocate and defender in public discussions – Thomas Huxley:

> When I reached intellectual maturity and began to ask myself whether I was an atheist, a theist, or a pantheist; a materialist or an idealist; a Christian or a freethinker; I found that the more I learned and reflected, the less ready was the answer; until, at last, I came to the conclusion that I had neither art nor part with any of these denominations, except the last. The one thing in which most of these good people were agreed was the one thing in which I differed from them. They were quite sure they had attained a certain "gnosis," – had, more or less successfully, solved the problem of existence; while I was quite sure I had not, and had a pretty strong conviction that the problem was insoluble.[8]

Most atheists, though, claim that we *can* know that God does not exist: various arguments, often from science, give us convincing evidence to think there is no God. Atheists believe that there is no God and that we can know this. This means I won't be talking about agnosticism. Nor will we consider what German theologian Karl Rahner calls *practical atheism*, "a lifestyle in which no (discernible) conclusions are drawn from the (theoretical) recognition of the existence of God."[9] The life of an atheist is not one in which God happens to be theoretically or practically absent, but one in which God is intentionally ruled out because he is thought not to exist.

Atheism in this sense is also simply more interesting. Just not believing in God may well reflect a more general skeptical attitude in life. If one moves from belief in God to agnosticism, God may not really be replaced with something else – his place may

---

[8] Thomas Huxley, "Agnosticism," in his *Collected Essays*, vol. 5, *Science and Christian Tradition* (London: Macmillan, 1893–1894), 239–240.

[9] Karl Rahner, "Atheismus II. Philosophisch–III. Theologisch," in *Lexikon für Theologie und Kirche*, vol. 1, *A–Baronius*, ed. Michael Buchberger, Josef Höfer, and Karl Rahner (Freiburg: Herder, 1957), 983.

be vacant, so to say. A sincere belief that there is no God is much bolder. As psychologists have convincingly shown if belief in God is actively rejected, it is usually replaced with something else; for instance, belief in progress may replace belief in divine providence, and belief in science may replace belief in revelation. Psychologists have argued that these things may provide the comfort and security that religion used to give.[10] Some atheists even go so far as to suggest that science can answer our moral questions, that is, that it can tell us what the good life is. Sam Harris's influential 2010 book *The Moral Landscape* aims to do exactly that. Positive atheists are more interesting than negative atheists because they have felt compelled to come up with alternative worldviews, such as existentialism, New Atheism, humanism, Marxism, and scientism.

What, though, are we talking about when we talk about god or God or gods? I take it that a god or a deity is a supernatural person who is thought to be worthy of worship. Of course, according to many religions, there is a multitude of supernatural persons: not only gods but also demons and angels. Gods are distinguished from demons and angels in that only gods are thought to be worthy of worship. Angels are to be revered and maybe prayed to, whereas demons are to be feared or exorcised. Only the gods are to be worshiped. The Greek god Zeus, the Scandinavian god Woden, the Sumerian god Enlil, the god of Islam, Allah, the Judaic god, Yahweh, and the Christian god, often referred to simply as "God" – that's what we are talking about. In this book, I will refer to several gods, but mostly to the god worshiped in the Abrahamic religions of Christianity, Islam, and Judaism.[11] Religious believers think God is perfect in every regard – omniscient, omnipotent, infallibly good, eternal, and omnipresent – and that he is the creator of the universe.

---

[10] See Miguel Farias, "The Psychology of Atheism," in *The Oxford Handbook of Atheism*, ed. Stephen Bullivant and Michael Ruse (Oxford: Oxford University Press, 2013), 472.

[11] I will refer to God with the words *he*, *him*, and *his* even though, of course, God is neither male nor female.

Atheists usually target belief in this particular god. I suppose that is because it is most widespread in Western democracy and theologically the most sophisticated: if belief in God has to go, then so does belief in all the other gods. If God, the eternal, perfectly good, and immaterial creator of the universe, doesn't exist, then surely Zeus, Woden, and Ganesha don't exist either.

Why Does Atheism Matter?

One may wonder why we should try to understand atheism. After all, many countries have relatively few atheists; in the case of the United States, they comprise even as little as 5 percent of the population. The vast majority of the world's population, some 80–85 percent, is religious. Admittedly, not all religious people believe in gods. Some Theravada Buddhists and Jains don't. Yet, most religious people believe in one god or another. Does it follow that atheism isn't that important? No, it doesn't – I think it's crucial to get more insight into atheism, its motivations, and its arguments.

Here's why. Atheism as I have defined it may be a minority position. Yet, many people nowadays live as atheists do. If atheism in the stronger sense is correct, then that would actually justify the kind of life that many people live – a life without God. In fact, many people nowadays tacitly rely on the stronger atheists. I think the idea is that these can do the challenging intellectual work for others, pretty much in the same way as many religious believers leave things like the details of doctrine and the relation between science and faith to a few specialists, such as religious scientists and clergy.

Atheism may be a minority position, but it is also the fastest-growing worldview since the beginning of the twentieth century, held by some 10 percent of the worldwide population now. Although the percentage of atheists may be low in the general population, it is much higher among students and faculty in colleges and universities, and these institutions shape the culture of the future.

In my own country, the Netherlands, for instance, the percentage of atheists in academia is as high as 35 percent.[12]

Religious people have additional reasons to take atheists seriously. For one thing, they share with them the idea that it matters whether or not God exists. Quite a few agnostics simply don't care whether God exists and don't think it particularly matters. In fact, some can rightly be called *apatheists*: they don't feel any affection or emotion (*pathos*) toward the whole issue. The fact that you've picked up this book suggests that you're probably not an apatheist. And in case you are, let's see whether that still holds once you've read this book.

Within the group of religious believers, Christians have even further reasons to try to better understand atheism. There are various passages in the Bible that seem to say that those who seek God sincerely will actually find him (e.g., Luke 11:9). To claim that all atheists are insincere seems implausible – in any case, that's a kind of suspicion and dehumanization that I don't feel comfortable with at all. So why is it that some atheists don't find God, even though they honestly seek him? In order to provide a satisfactory solution to this challenging problem, we need to better understand atheism.

There is something elusive about atheism. After all, unlike Christianity, Hinduism, or Islam, atheism as such does not have an explicit view of the world. It is merely the denial that there are any gods. It rules out something without thereby saying what reality is like. It is one thing to declare that God is dead; it's quite another thing to come up with an alternative story of why we are here, what makes something good or evil, and what provides

---

[12] For more numbers on atheists internationally, especially among academics, see Elaine Howard Ecklund, David R. Johnson, Brandon Vaidyanathan, Kirstin R. W. Matthews, Steven W. Lewis, Robert A. Thomson Jr., and Di Di, *Secularity and Science: What Scientists around the World Really Think about Religion* (Oxford: Oxford University Press, 2019); Elaine Howard Ecklund and David R. Johnson, *Varieties of Atheism in Science* (New York: Oxford University Press, 2021).

meaning in life.[13] As Nietzsche sharply noticed in a captivating aphorism, the death of God leaves a yawning void:

> God is dead! God remains dead! And we have killed him! Yet his shadow still looms. How can we console ourselves, the murderers of all murderers! The holiest and mightiest thing the world has ever possessed has bled to death under our knives: who will wipe this blood from us? With what water could we clean ourselves? What festivals of atonement, what holy games will we have to invent for ourselves? Is the magnitude of this deed not too great for us? Do we not ourselves have to become gods merely to appear worthy of it?[14]

How should one understand and assess a view that is primarily negative in its orientation? And what alternatives can it come up with? These are challenging questions that we need to address.

The Future of Atheism

Some people may object that understanding atheism is not all that relevant since atheism is on the decline. In a recent piece, blogger Scott Alexander argued that from 2005 or so onwards, public attention for atheism grew steadily and reached a peak around 2012.[15] Since then, attention has been withdrawn. He backs up this idea with large quantities of online data, such as the number of Google searches for "atheism," the use of the word *atheism* in the *New York Times*, and the number of visits to influential atheist websites, such

---

[13] Mikael Stenmark rightly draws attention to this feature of atheism in his "Secular Worldviews: Scientific Naturalism and Secular Humanism," *European Journal for Philosophy of Religion* 14, no. 4 (2022): 237–264.

[14] Friedrich Nietzsche, *The Gay Science*, ed. Bernard Williams, trans. Josefine Nauckhoff and Adrian Del Caro (Cambridge: Cambridge University Press, 2001), 120.

[15] See Scott Alexander, "New Atheism: The Godlessness That Failed," *Slate Star Codex* (blog), October 30, 2019, https://slatestarcodex.com/2019/10/30/new-atheism-the-godlessness-that-failed/.

as www.infidels.org and www.freethoughtblogs.com. In a significantly more speculative manner, he even goes on to provide an
explanation for this remarkable phenomenon:

> Most movement atheists weren't in it for the religion. They were
> in it for the hamartiology. Once they got the message that the
> culture-at-large had settled on a different, better hamartiology, there
> was no psychological impediment to switching over. We woke up
> one morning and the atheist bloggers had all quietly become social
> justice bloggers. Nothing else had changed because nothing else had
> to; the underlying itch being scratched was the same. They just had
> to CTRL+F and replace a couple of keywords.

A hamartiology is a theory or doctrine of *sin*: it explains what went
wrong with the world – how sin entered our lives – and, if we add a
bit of soteriology to it (the theory of salvation), also how the world
can be redeemed. The story line for New Atheism was that religion
is pretty much the root of all evil and that the world can be redeemed
if we adopt a secular, enlightened approach to life. Alexander suggests that that was only a superficially adopted story line and that
most of its advocates have now simply switched to social-justice
rhetoric. What went wrong were such things as racism, sexism, and
colonialism, and the world can be redeemed by social justice – for
example, ensuring equal pay for men and women, tackling racist
biases, and fighting such things as mansplaining and manspreading.

I doubt whether this is right. Sam Harris, Richard Dawkins, and
other leading atheists are well-known for fighting what they consider
to be the dangers of the woke movement. But even if it is right that
many movement atheists have simply moved on to social-justice
issues, does that mean the debate about atheism has become irrelevant? Surely not. First of all, it is not clear how we should interpret
these data. Take the fact that people use the search term "atheism"
less often. What does that mean? Well, it could mean pretty much
anything. Maybe people are less interested in atheism in general and
now care more about specific arguments for atheism. Maybe there

is less interest in atheism because there are more atheists. I, for one, never search "religion" or "Christianity" online. It simply doesn't follow from the data that atheism is on the decline.

It's also doubtful whether "most movement atheists weren't in it for the religion." Of course, it's true that the use of words like *sexism, racism, patriarchy,* and *white supremacy* has increased dramatically over the last 10 years, especially in such outlets as the *New York Times.* And many of the activists involved in, say, promoting equal pay and fighting racism may well have been heavily involved in the atheism-religion debate. Yet, nothing follows about their commitment regarding atheism either when they were debating atheism or when they are no longer debating it. Research shows that atheism continues to grow steadily in the United States and in other secular countries.[16] Even if atheists gave up the debate on atheism and turned to social justice (we have no exact numbers on that), there is no reason to think that that involved *giving up* atheism itself.

If the data about the online use of words like *atheism* are not to be explained in terms of the decline of atheism, then how *should* we interpret this development? Well, these data show that the so-called culture wars are getting less heated. New Atheism may merely be the pendant of Christian fundamentalism. The term *New Atheism* really caught on after the publication of Richard Dawkins's *The God Delusion* in 2006; its use peaked around 2012, and then it gradually declined. But New Atheism is only a rather extreme version of atheism, one that numerous atheists firmly distance themselves from. We will see in this book several examples of both New Atheism and the movement away from it.

There has also been radical development in internet culture anyway. Long pieces, blogs, and chats on various websites have been replaced with shorter exchanges on Facebook, Twitter, and other

---

[16] See, for instance, "In U.S., Decline of Christianity Continues at Rapid Pace," Pew Research Center, October 17, 2019, www.pewresearch.org/religion/2019/10/17/in-u-s-decline-of-christianity-continues-at-rapid-pace/.

social media. Another reason why the debate about New Atheism has withered away is that people at some point just get tired of the eternal repetition of the same points, examples, arguments, counterarguments, and counter-counterarguments. Atheism, after all, is primarily a negative idea in the sense that it first and foremost denies belief in supernatural entities. Therefore, it is somewhat limited in its conceptual resources. After so many years, the debate just gets predictable and boring for some people, and they move on.

Atheism has steadily grown over the last few decades. As Ariela Keysar and Juhem Navarro-Rivera conclude on the basis of a metastudy of recent statistical research on atheism worldwide:

> Positive atheism is gaining strength in many countries, with young and educated people, predominantly males, expressing sharp religious scepticism and breaking taboos against disbelief.[17]

One reason atheism will continue to find new supporters is that its main narrative is, by its very nature, attractive for curious people. It tells us that what most people believe and what is widely accepted turns out, on serious inquiry, to be a delusion, a myth, a phantasy of gigantic proportions. Not only that, most atheists boldly assert that *science* show this – and who would want to quibble with science? There's something exhilarating about this: one comes to see what most people in their ignorance or credulity have missed. A quick glance at the titles of some of the most influential atheistic books out there confirms that the main narrative of contemporary atheism is indeed a debunking story: *The God Delusion* by Richard Dawkins, *The End of Faith* by Sam Harris, *The Demon-Haunted World: Science as a Candle in the Dark* by Carl Sagan, *Breaking the Spell* by Daniel Dennett, *God: The Failed Hypothesis* by Victor Stenger, *The God Virus* by Darrel Ray, and *Why People Believe Weird Things* by

---

[17] Ariela Keysar and Juhem Navarro-Rivera, "A World of Atheism: Global Demographics," in *The Oxford Handbook of Atheism*, ed. Stephen Bullivant and Michael Ruse (Oxford: Oxford University Press, 2013), 583.

Michael Shermer. Of course, this narrative has old roots: Sigmund Freud already famously criticized belief in God in his 1927 work *The Future of an Illusion*. Atheism, then, is a growing movement with a particularly appealing PR strategy. It's here to stay, and we can only make progress by coming to better understand it.

Learning from Atheism

Many books about atheism aren't really about atheism, particularly when they are written by religious believers. They typically argue for belief in God or even for specifically Christian belief. Of course, if God exists, then atheism is false. American Christian author Eric Metaxas's book on atheism, *Is Atheism Dead?*,[18] for instance, is largely devoted to arguments for God's existence and provides historical and philosophical evidence in favor of Christianity.

Don't get me wrong: I think such arguments are fascinating and useful.[19] What I have in mind here are cosmological arguments, arguments from fine-tuning and from miracles, the moral argument, arguments from consciousness, and ontological arguments. These are all challenging arguments for the existence of God that have flourished over the last few decades, as we witnessed a true revival in the philosophy of religion. New empirical evidence from cosmology and physics that bears on these arguments, as well as new conceptual tools, such as modal logic, have been taken into account. The same holds for arguments for specifically Christian belief: these now take into account textual evidence, archaeological evidence, and other historical evidence. These arguments are not to be dismissed easily.

Yet, I find there is something deeply unsatisfactory about approaching atheism in this way. It isn't all that different from

[18] See Eric Metaxas, *Is Atheism Dead?* (Washington, DC: Salem Books, 2021).
[19] In fact, elsewhere I've delved into such arguments. See Stefan Paas and Rik Peels, *God bewijzen: Argumenten voor en tegen geloven* [Why it's OK to believe in God] (Amsterdam: Balans, 2013).

assessing political liberalism by giving arguments for conservatism. Why not zoom in on what atheists have got to say themselves? Why not listen to them to hear their stories, understand their motivations, and reconstrue the way they think?

This book is not meant to bash atheism. In our polarized times, there's already enough of that. On both sides of the atheism-theism debate, we find authors who are full of disdain, cynicism, and even rancor. Christopher Hitchens once said: "Now I am absolutely convinced that the main source of hatred in the world is religion and organized religion, absolutely convinced of it.... And I think it should be, religion, treated with ridicule and hatred and contempt, and I claim that right."[20] These venomous and polarizing words were met with loud applause. Religious believers can be equally vitriolic. Take how Baptist minister and author Ray Comfort blames all the evils of the world on atheism: "An atheist will lie to you and steal from you without qualms of conscience because he doesn't fear God. We have a generation who have given themselves to fornication, lying, theft and blasphemy. We have school shootings, violence, pornography, etc. and what's the common denominator? They lack the fear of God. Atheistic evolution completely removes God and moral accountability. This is a cancer that destroys a nation from the inside."[21] This New Zealand–born American evangelist has his own television show and reaches a large audience by way of numerous books and public debates. His comparing atheism to cancer is not an innocuous thing.

Clearly, this is not the way to go. Such approaches only serve to confirm what one already believes. I've been fascinated by atheism for more than 25 years now. Ever since I started reading atheist existentialists like Jean-Paul Sartre as a teenager, I've

---

[20] Hitchens said these things in a lecture at the University of Toronto's Hart House Debating Club in 2006; see www.youtube.com/watch?v=zDap-K6GmLo.

[21] See this 2009 interview with Ray Comfort by Mark Kelly: www.baptistpress.com/resource-library/news/atheism-ray-comfort-warns-of-its-results/.

been convinced there are crucial insights to be gleaned from the experiences and rigorous search for truth that we find in the work of various atheists. I therefore invite you to join me in my attempt to better understand the atheist, his motivations, and his arguments.[22] I believe we need this for improving the public debate about atheism and religion. Rather than denigrating or ridiculing atheism, I'll argue, as a religious believer myself, that there's much we can learn from atheism.

Finally, the ideas in this book are inspired by countless conversations I've had with atheistic friends and colleagues, some of whom are rather well-known in the debate on atheism and religious belief – for example, the Dutch philosopher Herman Philipse and the Belgian philosopher Maarten Boudry. In addition to that, I've consistently backed up my ideas with material that everyone can access: blogs, articles, books, public debates, and videos. I would encourage anyone who feels challenged by the ideas expressed in this book to check the evidence for themselves.

---

[22] I will speak consistently of the atheist in terms of *he*, *him*, and *his*. Of course, there are countless female atheists as well. But it is hard to deny that the majority of atheists are male.

2 | Motivations for Atheism

Arguments and Motivations

What motivates atheists? In other words, why are some people atheists? You might think there is a natural answer to this question: atheists are motivated by *arguments* for atheism. In fact, I myself thought this much before studying atheism in more detail. However, when I set out to scrutinize motivations for atheism more systematically, that quickly and radically changed. Some atheists seem indeed to be motivated by arguments, but the majority of them seem not to be.

It isn't all that surprising that atheists are not primarily motivated by the various well-known arguments for atheism. Compare atheists with Christians. Why do Christians believe in God? And why do they embrace the Christian story[1] – the idea that there is a God who created the world, that God is good and forgiving, and that God has saved them through the suffering, death, and resurrection of Jesus Christ? If you ask a Christian why they believe these things, they hardly ever come up with a series of arguments.[2] They might know one or two,

---

[1] Christian faith does not *require* belief, even though it sometimes comes with belief, as has been argued by Jonathan Kvanvig, *Faith and Humility* (Oxford: Oxford University Press, 2018); Daniel Howard-Snyder, "Markan Faith," *International Journal for Philosophy of Religion* 81, no. 1–2 (2017): 31–60; Daniel J. McKaughan, "Authentic Faith and Acknowledged Risk: Dissolving the Problem of Faith and Reason," *Religious Studies* 49, no. 1 (2013): 101–124; and others.

[2] This is also noted by atheists – e.g., A. C. Grayling, "Critiques of Theistic Arguments," in *The Oxford Handbook of Atheism*, ed. Stephen Bullivant and Michael Ruse (Oxford: Oxford University Press, 2013), 38–39.

and they may even be able to spell them out in some detail. Yet, their faith in God is based on something else. It is grounded in what they read in the Bible, in going to church, in different kinds of religious experiences, in prayer, in singing, in being overwhelmed by God's grace during liturgical meetings, in the religious testimony of people they trust, and, in some cases, in the value of a religious upbringing. Frequently, there is not even a clear basis: faith in God spontaneously and irresistibly arises. It seems some humans are simply hardwired to believe in God. This is also true for many believers in other faiths, such as Judaism, Hinduism, and Islam.

In fact, upon reflection, it seems that this is true for *all* the major things we believe in, like the equality of men and women, the value of honesty, the fact that we can actually know the empirical world, that we love, that we have attachments to other people, that human life has special value. These are things that we believe and that matter to us. Yet, we don't believe them on the basis of a bunch of arguments. Of course, if we pushed someone, they might offer arguments for these views. They will do so because they realize that whatever brought them to hold this position might not convince the other, whereas an argument might. However, they themselves never accepted these things on the basis of arguments. These beliefs are simply part of how they see the world. They hold these beliefs because they were raised that way, because the beliefs are common sense, because they have a deep-seated intuition that they are true.[3]

Thus, we all believe these things, and we do so on the basis of intuitions or the feeling that something is convincing, or possibly not on the basis of anything at all. This is especially true for a wide variety of what the Austrian-British philosopher Ludwig Wittgenstein

---

[3] And, as the American theologian James Smith has pointed out, in believing various basic things, we are deeply affected by cultural values and ideals. See James K. A. Smith, *Desiring the Kingdom: Worship, Worldview, and Cultural Formation* (Grand Rapids: Baker Academic, 2009). For common sense and religious belief, see also Rik Peels and René van Woudenberg, eds., *The Cambridge Companion to Common-Sense Philosophy* (Cambridge: Cambridge University Press, 2021).

calls *hinge propositions*: statements that make up the framework of how we experience and interpret the world. Arguments are possible within such frameworks, but these hinge propositions are not themselves the result of arguments. What Wittgenstein has in mind are such things as the idea that there is a material world around us, that we can actually know it, and that we are beings with consciousness.[4]

Now, if the most basic things we believe about reality are not based on arguments, then why would atheism be any different? After all, atheism is a comprehensive view about the world: there is no God; there are no gods; there is just the natural world. And usually, this comes with the view that there are no angels, demons, immaterial souls, and the like either. Atheism is a fundamental view about the nature of reality, and it would therefore be surprising if it were usually based on a series of arguments. Some atheists are fully aware of this and acknowledge it. Nicholas Everitt, for instance, says:

> I sometimes cannot help wondering whether my rejection of the arguments for theism is as much the product of a prior commitment to atheism as to an intellectual insight into their faults. F. H. Bradley famously remarked that "metaphysics is the finding of bad reasons for what we believe on instinct." I don't believe that the reasons ... which I have advanced for atheism are bad, but I do suspect that they support what I anyway believe on instinct.[5]

[4] The notion of a hinge proposition was first developed by Wittgenstein in his *On Certainty*, ed. G. E. M. Anscombe and G. H. von Wright, trans. D. Pauland (Oxford: Blackwell, 1969–1975). For more-recent analyses of hinge propositions, see Annalisa Coliva, *Extended Rationality: A Hinge Epistemology* (New York: Palgrave Macmillan, 2015); Duncan Pritchard, *Epistemic Angst: Radical Skepticism and the Groundlessness of Our Believing* (Princeton: Princeton University Press, 2015), 70; and Crispin Wright, "On Epistemic Entitlement II: Welfare State Epistemology," in *Scepticism and Perceptual Justification*, ed. Dylan Dodd and Elia Zardini (Oxford: Oxford University Press, 2004), 213–247.
[5] Nicholas Everitt, "How Benevolent *Is* God? An Argument from Suffering to Atheism," in *50 Voices of Disbelief: Why We Are Atheists*, ed. Russell Blackford and Udo Schüklenk (Oxford: Wiley-Blackwell, 2009), 21–22.

John Schellenberg is another example:

> Even if all of the arguments for atheism I have discovered after more fully surrendering to wonder, to the unexpected, to the fascinating strangeness of the world turned out to be unsound, I would remain a nonbeliever.[6]

Perhaps most up-front is the well-known American philosopher Thomas Nagel:

> I want atheism to be true and am made uneasy by the fact that some of the most intelligent and well-informed people I know are religious believers. It isn't just that I don't believe in God and, naturally, hope that I'm right in my belief. It's that I hope there is no God! I don't want there to be a God; I don't want the universe to be like that.[7]

Nagel doesn't just believe that there is no God – he *wants* atheism to be true and *hopes* that there is no God. Apparently, atheism has to do not only with arguments but also with hopes and wants.

Of course, if you ask them why they are atheists, they will give arguments. Similarly, one can give arguments for Christianity, theism, or the existence of the external world. But these views are normally not based on such arguments. And although such arguments may be interesting, it is more worthwhile to explore people's *true* motivations for atheism.

This is not to deny that atheists frequently *assert* that their atheism is based on arguments. This is not surprising, for atheists commonly claim that religions like Christianity and Islam are deeply irrational because they lack supporting arguments that hold water. Don't get me wrong: I'm not suggesting that atheists are insincere. Some atheists may simply be *mistaken* about why they are atheists. For it is not at all uncommon for humans in general to be a

---

[6] John Schellenberg, "Why Am I a Nonbeliever? – I Wonder ...," in *50 Voices of Disbelief*, ed. Russell Blackford and Udo Schüklenk (Oxford: Wiley-Blackwell, 2009), 31.

[7] Thomas Nagel, *The Last Word* (New York: Oxford University Press, 1997), 130.

little deceived about their true motivations when it comes to crucial things in their lives.

If people are not primarily driven by arguments in embracing atheism or Christianity, then in exploring the arguments for these views one might not be addressing the most important issue. In fact, if a public debate or conversation on such topics is limited to a discussion of arguments, the discussion might not even be taking place at the right level.[8] So, let's explore what really motivates the atheist.

Being an Independent Thinker

One of the most important drivers for atheism is the ideal of being an independent thinker. Atheists do not want to be subjected to any intellectual authority that tells them what they should do or believe or feel or even be. They want to think and explore life for them-selves. This makes life an *adventure* for the atheist, especially an intellectual one. And don't we all like a bit of adventure every now and then? The idea that there is a pre-established meaning and pur-pose for humans is something that many atheists will firmly dislike.

Take American philosopher Louise M. Antony, editor of the influential volume *Philosophers without Gods*. Here is her succinct description of how being an atheist embodies the ideal of being an independent thinker:

> We [atheists] have no sacred texts, no authorities with definitive answers to our questions about the nature of morality or the purpose of life, no list of commandments that cover every contingency and

---

[8] What are the ideas in this chapter based on? I provide a wide variety of sources: autobiographical books and collections of essays by atheists, video fragments from public debates (such as those of Reasonable Faith and The Veritas Forum), texts from websites advocating atheism, and examples that I've encountered in public debates and conversations with atheists myself.

dilemma. We can have no confidence, the evidence of history being as it is, that the truth will win out, or that goodness will triumph in the end. We have no fear of eternal punishment, but no hope, either, of eternal reward. We have only our ideals and our goals to motivate us, only our sympathy and our intelligence to make us good, and only our fellow human beings to help us in time of need. When we speak, we speak only for ourselves – we cannot claim inspiration or sanction from the Creator and Lord of the universe.[9]

We can distinguish several elements here:

- As an atheist, one is not subject to an intellectual authority that tells one how to live one's life.
- There's no reason to think that goodness will triumph, so life is one big adventure.
- The things that drive us are our own goals and feelings for our fellow human beings; beliefs about our fate in the afterlife do not influence our decisions.
- When an atheist expounds a view, he can be challenged by anyone to give reasons for that view; an appeal to inspiration from a transcendent source is illegitimate, and so it should be, of course, for everyone else.

American philosopher Anthony Simon Laden uses a rather vivid and exciting metaphor to describe what life really is like on atheism:

Our existence is thus one long walk on a tightrope over a yawning abyss and there is nothing to catch us should we fall into meaninglessness or isolation or even mere ordinariness. But that is exactly

---

[9] Louise M. Antony, "Introduction," in *Philosophers without Gods*, ed. Louise M. Antony (Oxford: Oxford University Press, 2007), xiii. Thus also Louise M. Antony, "For the Love of Reason," in *Philosophers without Gods*, ed. Louise M. Antony (Oxford: Oxford University Press, 2007), 51, 58; Daniel C. Dennett, *Breaking the Spell: Religion as a Natural Phenomenon* (New York: Penguin Group, 2006), 311; Kenneth A. Taylor, "Without the Net of Providence: Atheism and the Human Adventure," in *Philosophers without Gods*, ed. Louise M. Antony (Oxford: Oxford University Press, 2007), 163.

BEING AN INDEPENDENT THINKER

what I find so exhilarating about being an atheist. Life is up to us; there are no safety nets. That's a bracing thought. It's also a reason to live.[10]

Again, the idea here is that how we live our lives is up to us; no one should dictate the choices we make. As Richard Dawkins explains, it has to do with growing up – we must let illusions go, in order to reach knowledge and understanding:

Safety and happiness would mean being satisfied with easy answers and cheap comforts, living a warm comfortable lie. The daemonic alternative urged by my matured Devil's Chaplain is risky. You stand to lose comforting delusions: you can no longer suck at the pacifier of faith in immortality. To set against that risk, you stand to gain "growth and happiness"; the joy of knowing that you have grown up, faced up to what existence means; to the fact that it is temporary and all the more precious for it.[11]

Elsewhere, Dawkins straightforwardly encourages the reader to embark on this adventure: "The bold step into the frightening void of what seems improbable has turned out right so often in the history of science. I think we should take our courage in both hands, grow up and give up on all gods. Don't you?"[12]

As Ayaan Hirsi Ali, a Somali woman who fled to the West, explains, atheism makes this life far more adventurous and intense:

The only position that leaves me with no cognitive dissonance is atheism. It is not a creed. Death is certain, replacing both the siren-song of Paradise and the dread of Hell. Life on this earth, with all its mystery and beauty and pain, is then to be lived far more

---

[10] Anthony S. Laden, "Transcendence without God: On Atheism and Invisibility," in *Philosophers without Gods*, ed. Louise M. Antony (Oxford: Oxford University Press, 2007), 132.

[11] Richard Dawkins, *A Devil's Chaplain: Reflections on Hope, Lies, Science, and Love* (Boston: Houghton Mifflin, 2004), 13.

[12] Richard Dawkins, *Outgrowing God: A Beginner's Guide* (London: Bantam, 2019), 278.

intensely: we stumble and get up, we are sad, confident, insecure, feel loneliness and joy and love. There is nothing more; but I want nothing more.[13]

All of this squares well with what scientists have noted about atheism. According to Miguel Farias, what distinguishes atheists from other people is a *gnostic* drive: they strive for self-mastery by way of knowledge acquisition. This Portuguese-British psychologist argues that such self-mastery comes with competitive individualism, the desire to master oneself and to portray oneself as distinct from the rest of humanity. Moreover, atheists are generally sensation seeking: they try novel ideas, they are open to new experiences, they search intense and pleasurable sensations, and they are curious. These are all reflected in a wide variety of actions, such as sexual behavior.[14]

How should we think of this ideal of being an independent thinker? And does it point in the direction of atheism? I think believers should frankly admit that religious institutions, such as the church, have not always been safe places to pursue creative thinking and open-minded investigation to find the truth. In fact, some Christian leaders have actively discouraged such pursuits. Both in Roman Catholic and in Protestant churches, there have at times been unhealthy intellectual dependence, dogmatism, fear of new ideas, and ferocious debates about side issues in the Christian faith. Martin Luther famously talked about the freedom of a Christian:[15] I believe such freedom ought to include open-minded reflection.

---

[13] Ayaan Hirsi Ali, "How (and Why) I Became an Infidel," in *The Portable Atheist: Essential Readings for the Nonbeliever*, ed. Christopher Hitchens (Cambridge, MA: Da Capo, 2007), 477–480.

[14] See Miguel Farias, "The Psychology of Atheism," in *The Oxford Handbook of Atheism*, ed. Stephen Bullivant and Michael Ruse (Oxford: Oxford University Press, 2013), 475.

[15] See Martin Luther's 1520 tractate *On the Freedom of a Christian; Von der Freiheit eines Christenmenschen, De libertate Christiana*, ed. Reinhold Rieger (Tübingen: Mohr Siebeck, 2007).

The apostle Paul encouraged his readers to examine everything and to hold firmly to that which is good (1 Thess. 5:21). Acknowledging the faults made by the church and other religious organizations on this score creates room for an open discussion.

I also think religious believers ought to wonder to what extent they have abandoned certain fields of research. Take the philosophy of religion. Most philosophers, believers included, were so impressed with logical positivism that they simply gave up on all the hard questions in the philosophy of religion. Logical positivism says that religious statements and utterances, like all metaphysical claims, are literally meaningless. Consequently, even what looked like philosophy of religion wasn't really philosophy of religion. The devout Catholic Alasdair MacIntyre and – at the time – staunch atheist Antony Flew jointly edited a volume in 1955 titled *New Essays in Philosophical Theology*. But the book wasn't really about anything that religious believers believe in. It was merely about the language of religious sentences. Fortunately, ever since the 1960s, there has been a true renaissance of philosophy of religion, due to the devoted work of such Christian philosophers as William Alston, William Lane Craig, Alvin Plantinga, Richard Swinburne, Eleonore Stump, Peter van Inwagen, and Nicholas Wolterstorff. Any conversation, though, should begin with an honest acknowledgment that for some reason or other, religious believers, Christians included, have sometimes mistakenly abandoned fields of research.[16]

Now, let us consider the ideal of intellectual independence in some more critical detail. Exactly what does the atheist have in mind? This is an important question, for in social epistemology – the field that studies the social dimensions of knowledge – it has

---

[16] It used to be thought that entire academic disciplines were less popular among religious academics, but there is now ample reason to think that this is false: there is, for instance, no significant distinction between the natural and the social sciences when it comes to the religiosity among their practitioners. See Elaine Howard Ecklund and Christopher P. Scheitle, "Religion among Academic Scientists: Distinctions, Disciplines, and Demographics," *Social Problems* 54, no. 2 (2007): 289–307.

become increasingly clear that, inevitably, human beings are heavily dependent on others for what they know about the world.[17] Utter intellectual independence is a myth and also not particularly worthwhile. In acquiring various skills necessary for thinking independently – such as knowledge of logic, argumentation theory, and history, and acquaintance with philosophical concepts and theories, languages, and bodies of literature – one has to trust the testimony of others. The issue is not *whether* to rely on others – everybody does – but *whom* to rely on *with respect to what*.

We should also note that within many mainstream religious movements, there has traditionally been plenty of room to think critically. There is substantial evidence to support this claim. Many medieval Arabic *madrasas* (Islamic colleges) highly increased literacy among the larger population and taught logic, philosophy, geography, astronomy, and mathematics. Some of their scholars, such as Al-Ghazali, deeply influenced Western critical thinking. In addition, virtually all major universities in Europe and North America were founded by Christians. And they founded them *in accordance with* and arguably even *because of basic tenets of the Christian faith*, such as the idea that God has created the natural world in an orderly fashion and the conviction that humans have been created in the image of God, so that they can investigate and come to know all sorts of things about the natural world. At the outset of the project of university research, one of the ideals was even to restore the knowledge allegedly originally possessed and lost by Adam.[18]

---

[17] Some examples are Alvin I. Goldman and Dennis Whitcomb, eds., *Social Epistemology: Essential Readings* (Oxford: Oxford University Press, 2011); and Jennifer Lackey and Aidan McGlynn, eds., *Oxford Handbook of Social Epistemology* (Oxford: Oxford University Press, 2022).

[18] This has been argued in detail by Australian historian of science Peter Harrison. See, for instance, Peter Harrison, *The Fall of Man and the Foundations of Science* (Cambridge: Cambridge University Press, 2007), and Peter Harrison and Jon Roberts, *Science without God? Rethinking the History of Scientific Naturalism* (Oxford: Oxford University Press, 2019). For the American context in particular,

Finally, we can witness and even empirically study such relatively independent critical thinking in the lives of many religious writers, philosophers, theologians, scientists, poets, politicians, and artists. The list is endless, but here are some examples from the religious tradition with which I am most familiar, Christianity: in politics, Abraham Kuyper and Martin Luther King; in literary writing, Fyodor Dostoyevsky, Etty Hillesum, and Marilynne Robinson; in theology, Augustine, Dietrich Bonhoeffer, and Sarah Coakley. My list for science will be a little longer, because it's sometimes boldly claimed there is a conflict between science and religion. In mathematics, Blaise Pascal and Charles Babbage; in physics, Galileo Galilei, Nicolaus Copernicus, Isaac Newton, James Clerk Maxwell, Michael Faraday, and Robert Boyle; in evolutionary biology and biomedicine, former director of the National Human Genome Research Institute Francis Collins; in chemistry, Joseph Priestley; in genetics, Gregor Mendel; in botany, Asa Gray. Some, such as C. S. Lewis and Richard Swinburne, even *became* Christians *because* they dared to think critically and independently. Any serious empirical or historical inquiry will show that being creative and inquisitive is generally *encouraged* by many of the world's religions, including Christianity.

Following Heroes

Another motivation for atheism is somewhat similar to that of intellectual independence, but crucially different on one point. Here, people are motivated not by being intellectually independent but by following someone they admire. The two motivations are similar in that atheists often want to follow in the footsteps of someone who is thought to be intellectually independent.

see George Marsden, *The Soul of the American Academy: From Protestant Establishment to Established Nonbelief* (New York: Oxford University Press, 1994).

The way this works is pretty straightforward: one deeply admires, say, Friedrich Nietzsche or Bertrand Russell for their courage, their rhetoric, their intellectual power, or the specific ideas they put forward. However, their atheism is an inextricable part of their philosophies. Therefore, unavoidably, one will have to buy into their atheism as well.

Note the way many atheists portray themselves. They present themselves, for instance, as a daring scientist who is willing to take harsh reality for what it is. Rather than believing what they would wish to be true, they accept only that for which they have solid evidence, no matter how disappointing that may be. They describe themselves as people willing to sacrifice illusions and dreams to know reality as it really is. And – this is crucial – they invite the audience to trust them and to follow them in this relentless pursuit of truth. Thus, they often present themselves as seasoned heroes that others who are less experienced can follow. Such approaches are quite common among atheists. In his introduction to *The Atheist Guide to Reality*, American philosopher of science Alex Rosenberg writes:

> Science reveals that reality is stranger than even many atheists recognize. From the nature of the reality uncovered by science, consequences follow. This book is about those consequences. It provides an uncompromising, hard-boiled, no-nonsense, unsentimental view of the nature of reality, the purpose of things, the meaning of life, the trajectory of human history, morality and mortality, the will, the mind, and the self.[19]

Rather than leaving it to others to assess and characterize his view, Rosenberg does so himself. He makes clear from the very start that his atheism is not only thoroughly informed by science but also "uncompromising, hard-boiled, no-nonsense, unsentimental." The message is clear: embrace this view if you dare.

---

[19] See Alex Rosenberg, *The Atheist's Guide to Reality: Enjoying Life without Illusions* (New York: W. W. Norton, 2011), ix.

Is this a sound motivation for being an atheist? I have my doubts. One could just as well pick a hero with a theistic or even Christian background – for example, Augustine, Thomas Aquinas, Blaise Pascal, C. S. Lewis, Karl Barth, Dag Hammarskjöld, or, in our days, Alvin Plantinga, Francis Collins, Rosalind Picard, or Marilynne Robinson. In fact, it is not uncommon in religious traditions to do some "hagiography." It is no coincidence that Eric Metaxas's biography *Bonhoeffer: Pastor, Martyr, Prophet, Spy*[20] sold over a million copies in more than 20 languages: people long for examples that they can follow. In exceptionally challenging times – the last few years of the Second World War – Bonhoeffer developed a radically new ethics for a secular time, one that dared to diverge from mainstream utilitarianism, deontologism, and virtue theory.[21] The lives of theists and Christians can be as inspiring as the lives of atheists. The point here is this: the fact that some intellectual heroes are atheists is, as such, not a good reason to become an atheist oneself.

There may also be something slightly immature about slavishly following someone and blindly accepting his atheism because one admires that person's philosophy. Why should that make us buy into someone's atheism? It may as well be a reason to *reconsider* that person's philosophy. Or maybe the two can be separated after all. It's not at all uncommon to profit from insights in Heidegger's existentialist oeuvre but to reject his Nazism, to embrace Newton's work in physics but to reject his theological treatises, to buy into the results of the Human Genome Project but to denounce Francis Collins's religious motivation for it. If all this is possible, then it's probably equally feasible to profit from someone's philosophy without also embracing his atheism.

---

[20] Eric Metaxas, *Bonhoeffer: Pastor, Martyr, Prophet, Spy* (Nashville: Thomas Nelson, 2010).
[21] Dietrich Bonhoeffer, *Nachfolge* (Munich: Chr. Kaiser Verlag, 1937), translated by R. H. Fuller as *The Cost of Discipleship* (New York: Macmillan, 1966); *Ethics* (London: SCM Press, 1995).

Traumatic Experiences

Of course, atheists, like anyone else, are likely to suffer in this world. Many of them will have disappointing or even traumatic experiences. Here, one can think of serious diseases, pain, accidents, natural disasters, or being the victim of a crime. Sometimes, a religious education can be such a trauma that it leads to continuous pain and feelings of guilt.[22]

One may experience such terrible things oneself. Take Ayaan Hirsi Ali's horrible experience with female genital mutilation in Somalia:

> She caught hold of me and gripped my upper body in the same position as she had put Mahad [her sister]. Two other women held my legs apart. The man, who was probably an itinerant traditional circumciser from the blacksmith clan, picked up a pair of scissors. With the other hand, he caught hold of the place between my legs and started tweaking it, like Grandma milking a goat. "There it is, there is the *kintir*," one of the women said.
>
> Then the scissors went down between my legs and the man cut off my inner labia and clitoris. I heard it, like a butcher snipping the fat off a piece of meat. A piercing pain shot up between my legs, indescribable, and I howled. Then came the sewing: the long, blunt needle clumsily pushed into my bleeding outer labia, my loud and anguished protests, Grandma's words of comfort and encouragement. "It's just this once in your life, Ayaan. Be brave, he's almost finished." When the sewing was finished, the man cut the thread off with his teeth.[23]

Needless to say, this deeply traumatic experience almost inevitably influences any future assessment of religious practices.

One may also read or hear about others having such experiences. Stewart Shapiro, for instance, describes how his belief in God disappeared when he heard of a boy with a serious disease who had to

---

[22] See, for instance, Antony, "For the Love of Reason," 46.
[23] Ayaan Hirsi Ali, *Infidel* (New York: Free Press, 2007), 32.

live his entire life in a plastic bubble. This American philosopher says that when he heard this story on the radio, something in him snapped:

> One day in February 1984, I was driving and listening to a radio news story about David Vetter, otherwise known as the "bubble-boy." The announcer said that he had been born, twelve years before, with a condition, known as severe combined immune deficiency (SCID), that robbed him of the usual defenses against infectious diseases. Since any infection would prove fatal, David lived in a sterile environment, a plastic bubble. He had no physical contact with any living organism. Eventually, the defense was breached, and his doctors had to enter the bubble. David then hugged his mother for the first time, and died a short time later, thus prompting the news story that day.[24]

Shapiro does not describe how he constructed a plausible argument against God's existence from the bubble-boy's suffering and that of his parents. Rather, he explains how what remained of his belief in God simply disappeared upon hearing this story. Again, what motivates the atheist has often little to do with arguments.

Now, there may be something less than fully rational about many cases in which disappointing and traumatic experiences lead someone to embrace atheism. Why do people sometimes abandon their faith when something bad happens in *their own* life? What's so special about one's own life? Why wouldn't it count against God's existence if others suffer while it *does* count against God's existence if one is hit by disaster oneself? Of course, I don't want to suggest that we should be harsh on anyone. It's fully understandable that one finds it hard to believe in God when one has undergone traumatic experiences. It would be pedantic and insensitive not to

[24] See Stewart Shapiro, "Faith and Reason, the Perpetual War: Ruminations of a Fool," in *Philosophers without Gods*, ed. Louise M. Antony (Oxford: Oxford University Press, 2007), 3.

acknowledge this. But we should also realize that other people's pain and suffering count as much as ours.

One may reply that there *is* a crucial difference between one's own suffering and the suffering of others whom one doesn't know.[25] One may think, as American philosopher Eleonore Stump has suggested,[26] that the first-person knowledge or knowledge by acquaintance that comes with personal suffering provides a specific kind of evidence that one lacks in the case of mere factive knowledge of the suffering of others. I think this is right: you truly come to know something new, something you didn't know before, when, for instance, you lose your own child. Of course, you knew all along that the loss of a child comes with unparalleled suffering, but exactly what such suffering amounts to is something you come to know only when you experience it yourself. Perhaps this is similar to how descriptions of color can never give you the knowledge that actually seeing that color will give you. However, this more personal dimension of knowledge by suffering is usually not what is thought to rule out God's existence. Rather, it's the very idea that people suffer. After all, most atheists would stress that *everyone* has ample reason to reject the existence of God, whether or not they've personally experienced such terrible suffering.

Sometimes, such personal experiences are turned into an argument against God's existence. In that case, the argument can be explored, as various accounts of the place of evil and suffering in a Christian worldview do. However, in many cases, the experience of pain and suffering directly gives rise to atheism, without any detailed arguments. Criticizing what one takes to be the argument will then be of little use. After all, that person's atheism is not based on an argument in the first place. I hope that in such cases, we can all just take the time to be there and listen.

---

[25] I thank Max Baker-Hytch for drawing my attention to this idea.
[26] Eleonore Stump, *Wandering in Darkness: Narrative and the Problem of Suffering* (Oxford: Oxford University Press, 2010).

Being Overly Skeptical

Ever since the work of Aristotle, the notions of virtue and vice have played an important role in philosophy. Virtues and vices are fairly stable character traits that influence one's actions. Virtues are often the mean between two extremes. Trust, for instance, is the mean between gullibility and distrust, while courage is the mean between fear and hubris. Since Linda Zagzebski's book *Virtues of the Mind*,[27] philosophers have gone beyond the moral virtues and started to pay attention to *intellectual* virtues and vices. These have to do with a person's cognitive life, character traits, such as open-mindedness and thoroughness, and intellectual vices, such as dogmatism and obtuseness.

One important explanation for atheism, it seems to me, is that one can be overly skeptical, which is widely considered to be an intellectual vice.[28] Of course, I don't mean to say that all atheists display the vice of being overly skeptical. My point is merely that in *some* cases, this vice explains why someone is an atheist. It is virtuous to critically listen to others. The two extremes on both sides of this virtue are vicious: to blindly accept anything one hears and to be overly skeptical.

Here's how this works. The British mathematician William Clifford argued against religious belief, boldly claiming that "it is wrong always, everywhere, and for everyone, to believe anything upon insufficient evidence."[29] The American psychologist William James replied that the aim of cognition is twofold: to believe the truth and not to believe falsehood.[30] According to James, Clifford

---

[27] See Linda Zagzebski, *Virtues of the Mind: An Inquiry into the Nature of Virtue and the Ethical Foundations of Knowledge* (Cambridge: Cambridge University Press, 1996).

[28] Here, I have been inspired by Tim J. Mawson, "The Case against Atheism," in *The Oxford Handbook of Atheism*, ed. Stephen Bullivant and Michael Ruse (Oxford: Oxford University Press, 2013), 22–37.

[29] William K. Clifford, "The Ethics of Belief," in his *Lectures and Essays* (London: Macmillan, 1901), 163–205.

[30] William J. James, "The Will to Believe," in his *The Will to Believe and Other Essays in Popular Philosophy* (Cambridge, MA: Harvard University Press, 1979), 24.

was obsessed with the desire not to be mistaken, to avoid any kind of false belief, and this came at the expense of acquiring true belief. I think there may be an important kernel of truth to this: Could it be that some atheists are preoccupied and at times even obsessed with avoiding falsehood, sometimes at the cost of acquiring truth? Even atheists themselves often characterize atheism or naturalism as being concerned with avoiding falsehood. According to Thomas Clark, for instance, "the naturalist mainly wants not to be deceived, not to make errors of logic or method or assumptions when understanding the world."[31]

There is an intimate relation between atheism and skepticism. Many skeptical websites also advocate atheism.[32] Some people devote their entire lives to the two. Michael Brant Shermer, for instance, is not only a prolific science writer but also one of the world's most influential atheists, besides being the editor in chief of the magazine *Skeptic* and founder of the Skeptics Society, which has over 55,000 members. Various professional philosophers, such as Massimo Pigliucci and Maarten Boudry, write mostly about atheism and pseudoscience. In fact, there's empirical research that shows that atheists are more likely than religious people to believe in conspiracy theories, such as the *Da Vinci Code* conspiracy.[33] If that's right, that may be because they are too skeptical of commonly accepted stories and explanations, particularly in the religious realm.

Just to be clear: I think a healthy dose of skepticism is useful, and I agree we need rigorous work on the demarcation between science and pseudoscience. What I'm suggesting, though, is that skepticism

---

[31] Thomas W. Clark, "Too Good to Be True, Too Obscure to Explain: The Cognitive Shortcomings of Belief in God," in *50 Voices of Disbelief*, ed. Russell Blackford and Udo Schüklenk (Oxford: Wiley-Blackwell, 2009), 58.

[32] E.g., SkepticZone.tv, Skeptic.com, TheSkepticsguide.org, Skepticule.co.uk, and Skepsis.nl.

[33] See Anna-Kaisa Newheiser, Miguel Farias, and Nicole Tausch, "The Functional Nature of Conspiracy Beliefs: Examining the Underpinnings of Belief in the Da Vinci Code Conspiracy," *Personality and Individual Differences* 51, no. 8 (2011): 1007–1011.

can become a vice and that the obsession with anything that could go wrong belief-wise is a sign of that – in religion, in the debate on science and pseudoscience, in the paranormal realm, and in any other domain in life in which much nonsense can be found.

Some atheists go much further than this. John Gray, for instance, says that "while atheists may call themselves freethinkers, for many today atheism is a closed system of thought. That may be its chief attraction."[34] If he is right, another vice that leads some to atheism is *narrow-mindedness*, a closed system of thought that provides simple answers, excludes anomalies, and makes it much easier to leave other options aside. If Gray is onto something here, then paradoxically, there would be almost opposed ideals for atheism: the open-minded quest for truth as an independent thinker and the narrow-minded search for a closed, somewhat black-and-white system of thought. But I've seen people be attracted to religion for similar almost diametrically opposed reasons: some come to believe in God because of a rigorous open search for truth, whereas others fall for religious fundamentalism because it provides easy answers in an uncertain world. If it holds for religious people, why wouldn't it hold for atheists?

Caricatures of God and of Belief in God

Caricatures may also be a motivation for atheism. By *caricature*, I mean a picture, description, or imitation of God or belief in God in which certain characteristics are exaggerated and others oversimplified, often in order to create a comic or grotesque effect. Strictly speaking, it is not the caricature itself that is a motivation for atheism. Rather, it is the negative emotion – feeling repelled, nauseated, abhorred – toward the phenomenon that the caricature evokes. The negative emotion is often entirely justified. The problem is with the caricature.

[34] John Gray, *Seven Types of Atheism* (London: Penguin Books, 2018), 2.

We may note at least three kinds of caricatures when it comes to motivations for atheism: caricatures of believers, caricatures of the attitude of faith, and caricatures of God himself. Let's start with caricatures of believers:

- *Believers act morally merely because they expect or hope to be rewarded by God.*[35] This is, of course, a caricature: I, for one, take care of my children because I love them, not because I hope to be rewarded by God for doing so.
- *Believers think they are the only ones who have something valuable to say on good and evil; they believe they have a monopoly on morality.*[36] Although there will undoubtedly be believers who think such absurd things, they will probably be the exception.
- *Most religious believers refuse to critically reflect on their beliefs.*[37] The very point of many religious and particularly theological traditions is to do exactly that. Also, many religious believers have some doubts about what they believe precisely *because* they think through what they believe.

Here are some caricatures of the attitude of religious faith:

- True faith means taking the entire Bible literally, which results in a conflict with science.[38]
- Faith excludes rational thinking.[39]

---

[35] See, for instance, Antony, "Introduction," xiii. See also Matthijs van Boxsel, "Het christendom is geen morosofie, maar domheid zonder meer" [Christianity isn't some evidently absurd pseudoscience – it's plain stupidity], in *Leven zonder God: Elf interviews over ongeloof* [Life without God: Eleven interviews about nonbelief], ed. Harm Visser (Amsterdam/Antwerp: L. J. Veen, 2003), 162.

[36] See, for instance, Ronald Plasterk, "Juist onder religieuzen heerst een gebrek aan ethiek" [On the contrary, among religious people, there is a lack of ethics], in *Leven zonder God: Elf interviews over ongeloof* [Life without God: Eleven interviews about nonbelief], ed. Harm Visser (Amsterdam/Antwerp: L. J. Veen, 2003), 113.

[37] See Dennett, *Breaking the Spell*, 16–17.

[38] See Shapiro, "Faith and Reason," 8. Others suggest something similar; see Dennett, *Breaking the Spell*, 240.

[39] See Shapiro, "Faith and Reason," 6–10.

- "Faith is believing what you know ain't so," Mark Twain famously said.[40]
- According to Bertrand Russell, "it is thought virtuous to have faith – that is to say, to have a conviction which cannot be shaken by contrary evidence. Or, if contrary evidence might induce doubt, it is held that contrary evidence must be suppressed."[41]

We also find caricatures regarding God himself.[42] Here are two:

- God is a supernatural tyrant. In the Abrahamic religions, God's goodness is not allowed to be the object of discussion.[43]
- "If God exists, He is the most prolific abortionist of all."[44]

Now, I call these *caricatures* because there is often a kernel of truth in them. It is true, for instance, that some people of faith are believers merely because they hope to attain heavenly reward. It is a caricature, though, in that this characteristic is consequently exaggerated and applied to all religious believers. It is true that some holy scriptures say things about God that go contrary to our moral intuition – for example, his command to Abraham to kill his son Isaac, in Genesis 22. Yet, in various religious scriptures, such as the Talmud, people also question God about his actions and about what he fails to do. God's actions are not to be swallowed willy-nilly.

Caricatures like these can be intentionally embraced. But it isn't only atheists who sometimes do that. All humans are susceptible to doing this, say, in order to score points in a public debate. I've seen Christians portray adherents of evolutionary theory as proponents

---

[40] See his *Following the Equator: A Journey around the World* (Hartford: American Publishing Company, 1897), chap. 7, "Pudd'nhead Wilson's New Calendar."

[41] Bertrand Russell, *Why I Am Not a Christian* (London: Routledge, 1996), xxiii.

[42] I deem these the most important caricatures. There are, of course, further ones: those concerning the church (the mosque, etc.), holy scriptures, the history of religions, prophets, founders, and so on.

[43] Fernando Savater, *La vida eterna* [Eternal life] (Madrid: Mateu Cromo, 2007).

[44] Sam Harris, *Letter to a Christian Nation* (London: Bantam, 2007), 38.

of eugenics and other morally abhorrent positions, and even suggest a connection between evolutionary theory and the abject views about races put forward in the Third Reich. It would not be surprising, therefore, if a number of people embraced some of these caricatures while knowing full well that they *are* caricatures. However, in many other circumstances, they are the result of ignorance. Such ignorance can be culpable. For example, if any of the caricatures I mentioned above are put forward in a public debate, they are culpable: there is plenty of evidence to show that each of them is false, and we may expect a public speaker to delve into this material before presenting such faulty views. In other circumstances, especially personal conversations, one may not be culpable for them, or at least not as culpable. We live in a culture that perpetuates a wide variety of myths about God's character traits in traditions, about the nature of faith, and about what it is to be a believer, and it often is not easy for people growing up in such a secular society to dispel such myths.

I do believe there's value in assessing arguments for and against God's existence, but not in response to caricatures. After all, if plausible arguments for God's existence are given, but God is thought to be immoral, or religious faith is thought to come with the dismissal of reason, belief in God has not become more attractive at all. What is needed is a careful evaluation of such caricatures, drawing in historical, statistical, and textual evidence. Often, obstacles arising from caricatures need to be removed before a fruitful conversation can take place about the alleged truth of theism or atheism.

Moral Repugnance

Another motivation for atheism is moral repugnance toward God or toward religious believers. This is not another instance of a caricature. For in general, there is no particular exaggeration here. Rather, atheists are morally repelled by what religions actually say.

There is a long list of what atheists find morally repugnant in God. For instance, God chooses a specific people, Israel – this is not at all what one would expect from a morally fair God who created the entire universe.[45] God allows people to suffer in order to test them – a responsible person would never do that.[46] God commands all sorts of atrocities in the Tanakh, the Christian Bible, and the Qur'an.[47] If we take the Christian Bible seriously, we are to believe that God did morally reprehensible things, such as causing the innocent deaths of many children during a worldwide flood.[48] The Old Testament is full of atrocities and cruelties, and various atheists have been quick to point out that the New Testament doesn't do much better. Bertrand Russell is characteristically polite but also utterly clear when he says:

> You will find that in the Gospels Christ said: "Ye serpents, ye gen-eration of vipers, how can ye escape the damnation of hell?" That was said to people who did not like His preaching. It is not really to my mind quite the best tone, and there are a great many of these things about hell. There is, of course, the familiar text about the sin against the Holy Ghost: "Whosoever speaketh against the Holy Ghost it shall not be forgiven him neither in this world nor in the world to come." That text has caused an unspeakable amount of misery in the world, for all sorts of people have imagined that they have committed the sin against the Holy Ghost, and thought that it would not be forgiven them either in this world or in the world to come. I really do not think that a person with a proper degree of

---

[45] Joseph Levine, "From Yeshiva Bochur to Secular Humanist," in *Philosophers without Gods*, ed. Louise M. Antony (Oxford: Oxford University Press, 2007), 26.

[46] Antony, "For the Love of Reason," 57.

[47] Jonathan E. Adler, "Faith and Fanaticism," in *Philosophers without Gods*, ed. Louise M. Antony (Oxford: Oxford University Press, 2007), 285; Elizabeth Anderson, "If God Is Dead, Is Everything Permitted?," in *Philosophers without Gods*, ed. Louise M. Antony (Oxford: Oxford University Press, 2007), 219.

[48] Thus Walter Sinnott-Armstrong, "Overcoming Christianity," in *Philosophers without Gods*, ed. Louise M. Antony (Oxford: Oxford University Press, 2007), 72.

kindliness in his nature would have put fears and terrors of that sort into the world.[49]

Well-known for being a little less polite is Christopher Hitchens. He leaves no doubt about his moral attitude toward the idea that there is an omnipresent, all-powerful God:

> Reviewing the false claims of religion I do not wish, as some sentimental materialists affect to wish, that they were true. I do not envy believers their faith. I am relieved to think that the whole story is a sinister fairy tale; life would be miserable if what the faithful affirmed was actually the case. Why do I say that? Well, there may be people who wish to live their lives under cradle-to-grave divine supervision; a permanent surveillance and monitoring. But I cannot imagine anything more horrible or grotesque.[50]

There is also a lot about religious believers that many atheists find morally repugnant. Religious convictions lead to conflicts between people[51] and in some cases even to murder.[52] The history of the church is full of all sorts of atrocities, including the Crusades and the burning of witches by the Inquisition. The Roman Catholic Church has adopted a repugnant moral policy regarding artificial birth control (namely, forbidding it entirely), leading to the illness and death of millions worldwide. The church is a place where the freedom to express one's opinion is often lacking. And most abhorrent of all are the cases of child abuse in the church and the immoral attempts to cover them up.[53]

---

[49] Russell, *Why I Am Not a Christian*, 14. See also David Lewis, "Divine Evil," in *Philosophers without Gods*, ed. Louise M. Antony (Oxford: Oxford University Press, 2007), 232.

[50] Christopher Hitchens, *Letters to a Young Contrarian* (New York: Basic Books, 2001), 55.

[51] Sinnott-Armstrong, "Overcoming Christianity," 70.

[52] Sinnott-Armstrong, "Overcoming Christianity," 76.

[53] See Harm Visser, "Inleiding" [Introduction], in *Leven zonder God: Elf interviews over ongeloof* [Life without God: Eleven interviews about nonbelief], ed. Harm Visser (Amsterdam/Antwerp: L. J. Veen, 2003), 9.

There is something strange about this motivation for atheism. If religious believers are morally repugnant, that is a good reason to be morally weary when it comes to religion. But it clearly is *not* a good reason to think that there is no God.[54] Similarly, if God is morally repugnant, that is a good reason not to worship him. Christians believe that God is perfectly good. But if he is proven to be morally repugnant, then it would follow that God doesn't exist. Atheism, however, not only says that God doesn't exist. It says that *there are no gods whatsoever, whether good or evil.* Atheism would thus have to rely on something else besides God's alleged moral repugnance in order to be justified.

We should take moral repugnance seriously. And yet, we need to do more than just that. One thing that offers hope for progress is serious exegesis of relevant passages in holy scriptures. For example, did God really intend to have Abraham kill his son? Does he not forbid child sacrifice in numerous other passages in the Old Testament – for example, in Leviticus 18:21, Deuteronomy 12:31, and 2 Kings 21:6?

Here's an example that illustrates the need for careful exegesis. Richard Dawkins interprets the passage in chapter 11 of the book of Judges about Jephthah sacrificing his daughter as saying that God wants Jephthah to sacrifice his daughter:

Jephthah was horrified to remember his promise to God. But he had no choice. He had to cook his daughter. God was so looking forward to the promised smell of burning. His daughter very decently agreed to be sacrificed, asking only to be allowed to go into the mountains for two months first, "to bewail her virginity." After two months

---

[54] Some atheists have even noted as much – e.g., Graham Oppy, "Arguments for Atheism," in *The Oxford Handbook of Atheism*, ed. Stephen Bullivant and Michael Ruse (Oxford: Oxford University Press, 2013), 60. One might try to turn this into something of an argument; for instance, should we not expect Christians to behave morally better than nonbelievers, since they are closer to God if indeed there is a God? We return to that later.

she did her duty and returned. Jephthah kept his promise and bar-becued his daughter so God could have a nice, satisfying smoke.[55]

Of course, the point of the authors – yes, there were several of them – of the book of Judges is exactly the opposite. God does not seek any sort of human sacrifice at all. It is Jephthah and Jephthah alone who is responsible for the situation. He is an immoral leader who wrongly sacrifices his daughter. Let me give just two examples of recent Bible commentaries that point this out:

> Immediately following his reception of Yahweh's empowering spirit, Israel's "man of the hour" gets entangled in a faithless, foolish, and shameful vow to Yahweh. In this way, Jephthah contributes to the over-all configuration of descent from good judges (Othniel, Ehud, Debo-rah) in the direction of more problematic ones (Gideon, Samson).[56]

And:

> Admittedly, the text offers no explicit judgment, be it negative or positive. However, Jephthah's shock reaction, his gradually falling silent, YHWH's silence, and the mere fact of human sacrifice leave hardly any doubt that all this should be evaluated negatively.[57]

God is not the problem – Jephthah is. Thus, as Dawkins's unin-formed moral indignation shows, what is also needed is simply more information, more historical and exegetical knowledge about difficult scriptural passages.

Another suggestion I'd like to make is that we should carefully consider various doctrinal ideas in religions. Take the Christian notion that sin has infected *all* areas of life. This means our moral intuitions have also been infected. We therefore cannot fully trust

[55] Dawkins, *Outgrowing God*, 81–82.
[56] Richard D. Nelson, *Judges: A Critical and Rhetorical Commentary* (Bloomsbury: T&T Clark, 2017), 220.
[57] Klaas Spronk, *Judges*, Historical Commentary on the Old Testament (Leuven: Peeters, 2019), 351.

them; our moral feelings need sanctification as well.[58] The atheist will not, of course, share this view, nor will the agnostic. But that's not the point. The point is that it makes little sense to treat a narrative about a particular action of God in isolation. Believers may well agree that although such acts by themselves are morally troubling, they make more sense if we take further beliefs, dogmas, and traditions into account. It is wiser and fairer, then, to approach such narratives in their theological context.

Finally, let's not forget that a discussion about what is good and evil is part and parcel of religions, Judaism and Christianity in particular. Humans frequently even challenge God on this point. Entire books in the Tanakh, such as Job and Lamentations, are devoted to addressing pain and suffering, and even to pleading to God. It is not clear, then, why moral repugnance should automatically lead people to abandon their belief in God; there seems to be plenty of room for dealing with such feelings in religion itself.

Status and Possessions

So far, we've explored motivations for atheism that are neutral between worldviews. I mean that these are motivations that can be acknowledged by everyone as motivations for atheism. Yet, one might think there are also motivations that are likely to be acknowledged only from a theistic perspective and a Christian one in particular.

An important idea in Christianity is that one can become a Christian only if one is willing to give up certain things and follow Christ. This is already hinted at in the Old Testament: God is a god of the weak and the poor, a god of the widows and the orphans. In the New Testament, this is confirmed time and again. In Luke 9, for instance, we read:

---

[58] Elsewhere, I've spelled out this idea in some more detail. See my "The Effects of Sin upon Human Moral Cognition," *Journal of Reformed Theology* 4, no. 1 (2010): 42–69.

Then he [Jesus] said to them all: "Whoever wants to be my disciple must deny themselves and take up their cross daily and follow me. For whoever wants to save their life will lose it, but whoever loses their life for me will save it."[59]

Following Christ, according to the Christian story, means giving up a lot of what is dear to one:

"Truly I tell you," Jesus replied, "no one who has left home or brothers or sisters or mother or father or children or fields for me and the gospel will fail to receive a hundred times as much in this present age: homes, brothers, sisters, mothers, children and fields – along with persecutions – and in the age to come eternal life. But many who are first will be last, and the last first."[60]

To someone who has kept all the commandments, Jesus says:

If you want to be perfect, go, sell your possessions and give to the poor, and you will have treasure in heaven. Then come, follow me.[61]

It then reads: "When the young man heard this, he went away sad, because he had great wealth."

Now, according to mainstream Christianity, the path of following Christ is often a path downward, a road on which we learn to be humble and give up money, power, and possessions. I'm not saying all versions of Christianity embrace this idea – some kinds of prosperity gospel, for instance, clearly don't. But the mainline Christian view is entirely unambiguous. Dutch-American literary scholar and priest Henri Nouwen has aptly described this in his booklet *The Selfless Way of Christ: Downward Mobility and the Spiritual Life*.[62] He not only described it accurately but lived up to it by abandoning

---

[59] Luke 9:23–24 (New International Version; all subsequent citations are from this version).

[60] Mark 10:29–31.

[61] Matt. 19:21.

[62] Henri Nouwen, *The Selfless Way of Christ: Downward Mobility and the Spiritual Life* (New York: Orbis Books, 2007). See also Bonhoeffer, *Nachfolge*.

his professorship at Harvard University and living the rest of his life among the disabled in a L'Arche community.[63]

If it is true that this is a key part of the Christian message, then it isn't unlikely that some atheists are simply unwilling to give up their possessions, status, and other things they value, because it is difficult for *everyone* to give up these things, and many people, including religious believers, fail to do so. Of course, the matter is complicated, because many atheists are morally sensitive humans who lead good lives and who are willing to care for the poor and other disadvantaged without any theistic backing.

I think I need not say much about whether this can justify atheism – this motivation is clearly less than fully rational. It may be a practical reason not to become a Christian, but it is no reason to think that there is no God.

What does this mean for the public debate about the existence of God? Obviously, no one should ever use this idea against an opponent in a public debate on the existence of God. It would be arrogant and condescending to say that what one's opponent needs is conversion and that he should give up his possessions and status in order to follow Jesus Christ. In fact, any such line of reasoning easily becomes *ad hominem* or even manipulative. Yet, paradoxically, if the Christian story about the world is right (and we can't simply assume that it's false), then in some cases this narrative about status and possessions may be spot-on. Maybe, then, such motivations for atheism should be explored only in a much more personal context, in relations of trust and mutual respect.

Obstacles between God and Humans

A final motivation for atheism is another one that can play a role only from a religious perspective. In a conversation about God and

---

[63] For a description of that, see Jurjen Beumer, *Henri Nouwen: A Restless Seeking of God* (Chicago: Independent Publishing Group, 1999).

whether to believe in God or not, though, it makes perfect sense to consider factors that might play a role from an atheistic perspective as well as factors that might play a role from a religious perspective. We should go where the evidence leads. The idea is that there can be certain relational obstacles between God and humans. Such obstacles may make it hard or even impossible for the atheist to meet God even if he sincerely seeks God. Obviously, the idea is not that this will make it impossible *for God* to find the atheist. Rather, the idea is that relational obstacles may stand in the way between the atheist and God and that God may decide not to reveal himself for the time being – for instance, because the atheist should ask someone for forgiveness, or because he should forgive someone. God can have a multitude of reasons for not (yet) revealing himself to someone.[64]

On Christianity, this is not merely a logical possibility or a speculation. Several texts from the Old and New Testaments show that we need to take this option seriously. In his Sermon on the Mount, Jesus says at some point:

> Therefore, if you are offering your gift at the altar and there remember that your brother or sister has something against you, leave your gift there in front of the altar. First go and be reconciled to them; then come and offer your gift.[65]

Note that this is not one of the lesser-known temple laws or regulations. Rather, it's counsel that Christ himself gives to his followers. Jesus seems to give this advice so that his followers don't worship God without also seeking to live in peaceful relationships with the people around them. He tolerates no such hypocrisy. Now, if Christianity is true, it is not at all impossible that God acts on this by withdrawing his presence when people fail to abide by this

---

[64] This is rightly pointed out by Leslie D. Weatherhead, *How Can I Find God?* (London: Hodder & Stoughton, 1933), 103–124.

[65] Matt. 5:23–24.

commandment, as he withdraws his presence frequently in the Bible when people seek God while doing injustice to their neighbors.

The issue of personal relationships and forgiveness is, of course, highly delicate. It has to do with personal hurt, suffering, anger, hope, and love. I therefore take it that exactly how distorted personal relationships could stand in the way between a person and God is, again, only aptly explored in a personal context. The proper place is not a public debate but a more intimate sphere of trust and mutual respect.

More to Come

So far, we've explored a number of motivations for atheism. In fact, they can be either *explicit motivations* or *tacit motives*. By that I mean that they can motivate one willingly and consciously – for instance, when some person realizes he is an atheist because he seeks adventure and excitement in life and takes that to rule out a religious approach to life. They can also be tacit and unconscious motives. In such cases, they motivate someone to be an atheist without that person being fully aware of that. You can be morally or aesthetically repelled by religious practices while failing to realize that that is your primary driver for atheism.

I've selected these motivations and motives because they occur widely and I feel comfortable as a philosopher and theologian to address them. This is not to say that there might not be *other* motivations for atheism. The thing is that these other motivations have already been addressed extensively by others. And in some cases, they require the expertise of a psychologist or psychiatrist rather than the reflections of a philosopher. If you'd like to delve deeper into this, though, here are some of them:

- Many people feel that religion is losing more and more terrain to science. I believe this is false, but it sometimes takes a while before a myth is dispelled. In any case, this is a remarkable motivation, for obviously, even if religion were losing terrain to science, it isn't clear at all how atheism would follow. It would warrant at most some kind of agnosticism, because from the fact that science can explain things that were traditionally explained by religion, it obviously does not follow that there is no God.

- It is well-known that we all suffer from peer pressure. It is rather tempting to aim – consciously or unconsciously – to be like one's peers. Clearly, academics are no exception. It may be that many people are atheists simply because their peers are atheists.

- Atheists may experience some kind of aesthetic repugnance vis-à-vis what they can think of as the chaotic and unpleasantly emotional nature of some religious gatherings. They may not mind being guided through the liturgy by the world-famous choir of New College Oxford, but they might plainly dislike more chaotic and, music-wise, less-refined church services. Having felt unconformable at some religious gatherings myself, I don't find it difficult to imagine that aesthetic experiences can weigh in.

- Some empirical scientists have argued that there is a correlation between atheism and autism.[66] According to them, atheists are more likely to suffer from autism than nonatheists. The idea is that autism comes with difficulties in understanding what goes on in other people's minds and that this may lead to deficiencies when it comes to belief in God. I hasten to add that others have argued there's no such correlation.[67] I leave it to the psychologists to settle this debate.

[66] See Ara Norenzayan, Will M. Gervais, and Kali H. Trzesniewski, "Mentalizing Deficits Constrain Belief in a Personal God," *PLoS ONE* 7, no. 5 (2012): e36880.

[67] E.g., Leif Ekblad and Lluis Oviedo, "Religious Cognition among Subjects with Autism Spectrum Disorder (ASD): Defective or Different?," *Clinical Neuropsychiatry* 14, no. 4 (2017): 287–296.

- Paul Vitz has argued by way of a qualitative study that a dispro-
portionate number of atheists suffer from a distorted relationship with their father.[68] I think the approach of this American
psychologist is compatible with taking the arguments on both
sides seriously. I don't see why it would be perfectly legitimate for an atheist to explore to what extent, say, father issues
play a role in shaping one's image of God (as Sigmund Freud
famously argued), while it would be illegitimate for theists
(and others) to study how psychological factors influence atheistic belief.

I conclude there is a wide variety of motivations for atheism that
are not in any way arguments for atheism. I'm not, of course, saying
that *all* atheists are motivated by these. Rather, I suggest they may
frequently be motivations for atheism. If, as I have tried to show,
these motivations often play a crucial role in forming and shaping
atheistic belief, the time has come to take them seriously. We need
to do so if we truly seek to understand atheism. We should study
them in detail and take them into account in public debates and
personal conversations.

---

[68] See Paul C. Vitz, *Faith of the Fatherless: The Psychology of Atheism* (Dallas:
Spence, 1999).

3 | Atheistic Frameworks

Ways of Thinking

We encountered a large number of different motivations for atheism in the previous chapter. And later on in this book, we'll have a look at arguments for atheism. But there's something else that might lead one to reject God's existence, namely, one's *cognitive framework*. Cognitive frameworks are all-encompassing ways of thinking that lead you in a particular direction. If you adopt one of them, let alone several of them, you may well end up being an atheist. Discussing arguments for and against the existence of God won't make much of a difference in such a situation. To truly assess the intellectual solidity of atheism, we will have to delve into these frameworks.

Here's an example of what I have in mind. In a conversation between the "four horsemen of atheism" – Christopher Hitchens, Richard Dawkins, Sam Harris, and Daniel Dennett – Dawkins says:

> Religion, by embarrassing contrast, has contributed literally zero to what we know, combined with huge hubristic confidence in the alleged facts it has simply made up.[1]

Here, the idea is that religion is primarily about contributing to our knowledge, adding further facts to what we already know. If it doesn't do that, then it's worthless. Dawkins is, of course, right that religion

---

[1] See Christopher Hitchens, Richard Dawkins, Sam Harris, and Daniel Dennett, *The Four Horsemen: The Conversation That Sparked an Atheist Revolution* (New York: Random House, 2019), 19.

claims to know certain things, including alleged facts, such as the resurrection of Jesus Christ. And those knowledge claims matter. But religion can be valuable in a myriad of other ways: providing sense and meaning to our lives, doing justice to our experiences of good and evil, of ugliness and beauty in the world, and providing orientation in life, maybe even a relationship with God. A framework within which something is valuable only if it enhances our knowledge is not fruitful, then. Fortunately, it's also quite rare. But other frameworks are widely accepted. What are they, and what should we make of them?

Evidentialism

One important cognitive framework is called *evidentialism*. It is the widespread idea that belief in God is justified only if it is based on sufficiently strong arguments.[2] Thus, belief in God can be rational only if there are convincing arguments for God's existence. Such evidentialism is often implicit. Take what Australian philosopher John L. Mackie says in the conclusion of his influential book *The Miracle of Theism*:

> We can agree with what Laplace said about God: we have no need of that hypothesis. This conclusion can be reached by an examination precisely of the arguments advanced in favour of theism, without even bringing into play what have been regarded as the strongest considerations on the other side, the problem of evil and the various natural histories of religion. When these are thrown into the scales, the balance tilts still further against theism.[3]

---

[2] See, for instance, Daniel C. Dennett, "Thank Goodness!," in *Philosophers without Gods: Meditations on Atheism and the Secular Life*, ed. Louise M. Antony (Oxford: Oxford University Press, 2007), 116; Daniel Garber, "Religio Philosophi," in *Philosophers without Gods*, ed. Louise M. Antony (Oxford: Oxford University Press, 2007), 32–40.

[3] John L. Mackie, *The Miracle of Theism: Arguments for and against the Existence of God* (Oxford: Clarendon, 1982), 253.

The background assumption here, which goes entirely unquestioned, is that the tenability of belief in God depends completely on the arguments for God's existence. It's tempting to go along with this framework and seek arguments in favor of God's existence. But the problem with that response is that it suggests the rationality of belief in God does indeed depend on such arguments. This may be right, but we can't simply assume that it is. Soon after Mackie wrote these words, many philosophers of religion started to argue that evidentialism is in trouble. Reformed epistemologists like William Alston,[4] Alvin Plantinga,[5] and Nicholas Wolterstorff[6] have given various accounts of how belief in God could be rational even if there are no arguments for the existence of God: by way of mystical or other religious experiences, by way of a *sensus divinitatis* (a God-created belief-producing mechanism), or as a properly basic belief. We will later see what the arguments exactly look like. One might, of course, disagree with these arguments against evidentialism. But the point here is that we're easily seduced into going along with the atheist and delving into a debate about the arguments for and against God's existence, while really we should be asking a preliminary question that is often overlooked: Why should we think in the first place that belief in God is rational only if it is based on arguments?[7]

Distantionism

Another framework is the idea that you should avoid prayer, not participate in liturgy, and abstain from Bible reading in order to

---

[4] See William P. Alston, *Perceiving God: The Epistemology of Religious Experience* (Ithaca: Cornell University Press, 1991).

[5] See Alvin Plantinga, *Warranted Christian Belief* (New York: Oxford University Press, 2000).

[6] See Nicholas Wolterstorff, "Can Belief in God Be Rational If It Has No Foundations?," in *Faith and Rationality: Reason and Belief in God*, ed. Alvin Plantinga and Nicholas Wolterstorff (Notre Dame: University of Notre Dame Press, 1983), 135–186.

[7] As Tim Mawson puts it, we should ask what the underlying ethics of belief is. See Tim J. Mawson, "The Ethics of Believing in God," *Think* 9, no. 25 (2010): 93–100.

assess objectively the available evidence for God. The philosopher Daniel Garber, for instance, says:

> I may know that *if* I subject myself to a certain regimen (i.e., engage in religious practices), then eventually I will attain a state in which I will believe in God, and I will believe that my belief is rational. But that isn't good enough. From my present point of view, it looks too much like intentional self-delusion.[8]

Let us call this framework *distantionism*: in order to objectively assess, say, the Christian faith, you ought to distance yourself from it and evaluate what is to be said for and against it rather than engaging in prayer, rituals, Bible reading, worship, and other religious practices. The basic idea of distantionism is that belief in God is like conspiracy theories: if you read enough of them, you start to believe in them. Here, one might be reminded of the wager of the famous French philosopher and mathematician Blaise Pascal. He argued that, given the potential gains and losses involved, it is probably more prudent to act as if God exists and, thus, try to bring about belief in God. He explicitly addressed the worry that one might not be able to simply choose to believe that God exists:

> At least learn your inability to believe, since reason brings you to this, and yet you cannot believe. Endeavour then to convince yourself, not by increase of proofs of God, but by the abatement of your passions. You would like to attain faith, and do not know the way; you would like to cure yourself of unbelief, and ask the remedy for it. Learn of those who have been bound like you, and who now stake all their possessions. These are people who know the way which you would follow, and who are cured of an ill of which you would

---

[8] Garber, "Religio Philosophi," 39. See also Jonathan E. Adler, "Faith and Fanaticism," in *Philosophers without Gods*, ed. Louise M. Antony (Oxford: Oxford University Press, 2007), 280–281; Dennett, "Thank Goodness!," 115. For the legitimacy of various belief-influencing religious practices, see also John Cottingham, *Philosophy of Religion: Towards a More Humane Approach* (Cambridge: Cambridge University Press, 2014).

be cured. Follow the way by which they began; by acting as if they believe, taking the holy water, having masses said, etc. Even this will naturally make you believe, and deaden your acuteness.[9]

This might indeed sound to some like self-manipulation: because of the stakes involved, one should try to bring about belief in God in various ways.

Yet, one might doubt whether the cognitive framework of distantionism holds water. Why should we think that all evidence is to be had by way of construing arguments? Why not think that there is also nonargumentative evidence that can be obtained (even given to one) by way of such things as prayer, reading the Bible, and engaging in religious rituals? As various theologians and philosophers of religion stress,[10] belief in God is not at all like a scientific hypothesis – it is more like, say, the belief that your spouse loves you, the knowledge that Johannes Vermeer's painting *The Milkmaid* is beautiful, or the belief that your friendship is flourishing. If you distance yourself from your spouse or your friend, you will lack crucial evidence for your belief. Or compare it to tasting certain foods or listening to certain kinds of music: you will learn to appreciate these things only if you try them.

Another consideration regarding distantionism is of a more religious nature. The church has always stressed that we live in a sinful, broken world. Evil has also affected our cognitive faculties. Therefore, part of the evidence for God's existence is to be found only by actually obeying God, by living the life of faith.[11] Some philosophers, for instance, have recently argued that participating in the liturgy

---

[9] Blaise Pascal, *Thoughts*, trans. W. F. Trotter, in *Thoughts and Minor Works*, The Harvard Classics, vol. 48 (New York: Collier, 1910), 86, sect. 3, n. 233.

[10] E.g., Peter van Inwagen, "Is God an Unnecessary Hypothesis?," in *God and the Ethics of Belief: New Essays in Philosophy of Religion*, ed. Andrew Dole and Andrew Chignell (Cambridge: Cambridge University Press, 2005), 131–149.

[11] Thus also Leslie D. Weatherhead, *How Can I Find God?* (London: Hodder & Stoughton, 1933), 31–55. For a more detailed account of the cognitive consequences of sin, see my "The Effects of Sin upon Human Moral Cognition," *Journal of*

of religious gatherings may well be an important way of getting to know God.[12] On this view, "objectively" assessing the evidence while not engaging in a religious life will never do. Now, one may of course disagree with this. Still, there is no reason to just take the framework of distantionism for granted. There are alternatives to the idea that one should always distance oneself from the evidence.

Scientism

By far the most important and complex atheistic cognitive framework of our days is *scientism*.[13] It comes in many guises, but the main idea is that only the natural sciences lead to knowledge. The humanities do not, nor do common sense, religious experience, moral intuition, and the like.[14] Closely related versions say that the sciences provide knowledge about anything that can possibly be known, that there are no principled limits to science, that science can solve any problem, or that science provides the best knowledge.[15] Friends of scientism point to the impressive history of natural science in support of their scientism.[16]

Reformed Theology 4, no. 1 (2010): 42–69, and my "Sin and Human Cognition of God," *Scottish Journal of Theology* 64, no. 4 (2011): 390–409.

[12] See the many writings of Nicholas Wolterstorff and Terence Cuneo on the philosophy of liturgy, such as Wolterstorff's *The God We Worship: An Exploration of Liturgical Theology* (Grand Rapids: Eerdmans, 2015).

[13] Some things I say here about scientism are based on my "Scientism and Scientific Fundamentalism: What Science Can Learn from Mainstream Religion," *Interdisciplinary Science Reviews* (2022). https://doi.org/10.1080/03080188.2022.2152246.

[14] For a detailed exchange between proponents and opponents of scientism, see Jeroen de Ridder, Rik Peels, and René van Woudenberg, eds., *Scientism: Prospects and Problems* (New York: Oxford University Press, 2018).

[15] For an overview of these different kinds of scientism, see my "A Conceptual Map of Scientism," in *Scientism: Prospects and Problems*, ed. Jeroen de Ridder, Rik Peels, and René van Woudenberg (New York: Oxford University Press, 2018), 28–56.

[16] I explain this line of reasoning a bit more in "Ten Reasons to Embrace Scientism," *Studies in History and Philosophy of Science Part A* 63 (2017): 11–21.

When they talk about *science*, proponents of scientism have the natural and life sciences and their methods in mind: biology, physics, chemistry, earth science, and astronomy. These are to be contrasted with the social sciences, such as sociology, economics, management science, political science, psychology, and anthropology. And of course, they are to be distinguished from the humanities, such as linguistics, history, archaeology, and philosophy. The further one gets from the natural sciences and their methods, the lower the chances of acquiring knowledge.

Here is what American historian of science William Provine says about what follows from science:

> Modern science directly implies that the world is organized strictly in accordance with mechanistic principles. There are no purposive principles whatsoever in nature. There are no gods and no designing forces that are rationally detectable.... Modern science directly implies that there are no inherent moral or ethical laws, no absolute guiding principles for human society.... Human beings are marvelously complex machines.... When we die, we die and that is the end of us.... Free will as it is traditionally conceived – the freedom to make uncoerced and unpredictable choices among alternative possible courses of action – simply does not exist.... There is no ultimate meaning for humans.[17]

Of course, the mechanistic approach to science is now thoroughly outdated. In fact, it was already obsolete at the time Provine wrote these words. Quantum mechanics and general and special relativity have shown that our physical world is *not* organized strictly in accordance with mechanistic principles: randomness, chance, bilocation, and other nonmechanistic phenomena are all over the place. But that's not the point I'd like to make here. The point is that this quote shows how scientism works: it takes it that science

---

[17] William Provine, "Evolution and the Foundations of Ethics," *Marine Biology Laboratory Science* 3 (1988): 27–29.

has debunked core tenets of common sense and some other widely shared beliefs. Science entails there are no purposive principles in nature, no gods, no moral laws, no guiding principles, and that there is no free will, no ultimate meaning, no life after death. Clearly, science is the arbiter of truth. All other alleged sources of knowledge are unreliable.

It is important to pay attention to scientism in conversations on atheism. After all, if scientism is true, it is only natural to think there is no God. William Provine takes it that science *implies* that there are no gods or other designing forces – even though he fails to explain how science is supposed to imply that. There are various ways to go here. Take what Thomas W. Clark says, another adherent of scientism and director of the Center for Naturalism:

> The traditional Abrahamic god, a prime exemplar of the supernatural, is a patently *unexplained explainer* and thus necessarily absent from an ontology driven by the demand for explanatory transparency. Whether God is brought in to explain the creation of the universe or the design of life, in neither case can the supernaturalist provide an account of God's nature or how he operates. But good explanations don't simply posit the existence of some entity or process to fill a purported explanatory gap, in this case a creative, designing intelligence; they must supply considerable additional information to achieve explanatory adequacy. A good theistic explanation would have to supply concrete specifications for God – his motives, characteristics, powers, and modes of operation – to shed light on how and why he created certain species and not others, for instance.[18]

The idea Clark advocates here is that any explanation should be rigorously formulated in terms of properties, modes of operation,

---

[18] Thomas W. Clark, "Too Good to Be True, Too Obscure to Explain," in *50 Voices of Disbelief: Why We Are Atheists*, ed. Russell Blackford and Udo Schüklenk (Oxford: Wiley-Blackwell, 2009), 59–60.

motives, and so on. Thus, it seems we should believe in something only if it plays an indispensable role in a scientific explanation. This shows how close the relation between atheism and scientism is. One first adopts some kind of scientism, in this case, one that says we should believe in something only if it is needed for a scientific explanation. And then one shows that something, say, belief in God, is not needed for any kind of scientific explanation. Exit God. It will be obvious that in such a case, one can only assess a person's atheism by looking at their scientism.

British-Australian philosopher J. J. C. Smart is quick to apply the point to other religious beliefs, such as belief in miracles:

> It is easy to discount the miracle stories (including those of the resurrection) when one comes to see plausibility in the light of total science as the best touchstone of truth…. One should use the scientific method. Faith cannot do the job.[19]

The methods of science are the only legitimate methods – faith surely isn't one. If scientism is true, then belief in God, belief in angels and demons, and belief in resurrection and other miracles can be dealt with swiftly: science gives us no reason to believe in them, so they are out the door.

As Dutch philosopher Jeroen de Ridder has argued extensively, scientism has deeply influenced popular science writing.[20] Scientism, then, is not just a position in the ivory tower of academia – it is everywhere in public debates on atheism and belief in God. We can only truly understand why atheists so firmly reject God's existence if we come to better understand scientism.

Let me put my cards on the table. I love science. I admire its rigor, its patience, its ambition, and its self-critical attitude. I laud its communal nature, spanning across the centuries and across the

[19] J. J. C. Smart, "The Coming of Disbelief," in *50 Voices of Disbelief*, ed. Russell Blackford and Udo Schüklenk (Oxford: Wiley-Blackwell, 2009), 48–49.

[20] See Jeroen de Ridder, "Science and Scientism in Popular Science Writing," *Social Epistemology Review and Reply Collective* 3, no. 12 (2014): 23–39.

globe. It has given us incomparable insight into the natural world surrounding us, the universe, and our own bodies. And it has contributed greatly to a safer and more humane life for billions of people. It remains a fallible human endeavor, but it's undoubtedly one of the greatest achievements of humanity. Scientism appeals to science but is crucially different: it is a philosophical claim about the scope of science. The issue here is not whether science is valuable but whether scientism is tenable.

Bold and Modest Scientism

When we explore scientism in further detail, it is helpful to distinguish between modest and bold versions. Modest scientism says that only science provides knowledge *in a particular domain of life* – that's what makes it at least relatively modest. Take what Richard Dawkins says about the domain of answering the big questions of life:

> We no longer have to resort to superstition when faced with the deep problems: Is there a meaning to life? What are we for? What is man? After posing the last of these questions, the eminent zoologist G.G. Simpson put it thus: "The point I want to make now is that all attempts to answer that question before 1859 are worthless and that we will be better off if we ignore them completely."[21]

All attempts to answer these big questions before the publication of Darwin's *On the Origin of Species* are worthless, according to Dawkins: only biology can help us here. Or consider what British molecular biologist Francis Crick, who discovered the double-helix structure of DNA, claims about the domain of understanding ourselves: "You, your joys and your sorrows, your memories and your ambitions, your sense of personal identity

---

[21] Richard Dawkins, *The Selfish Gene*, 2nd ed. (Oxford: Oxford University Press, 1989), 1.

and free will, are in fact no more than the behavior of a vast assembly of nerve cells and their associated molecules."[22] Well, if we are just a bunch of cells, only chemistry and biology can help us understand ourselves. In addition, Dutch neuroscientist Dick Swaab addresses the issue of freedom: "Our current knowledge of neurobiology makes it clear that there's no such thing as absolute freedom.... The only individuals who are still free to a degree (apart from their genetic limitations) are fetuses in the early stages of gestation."[23] Again, only science, neurology in particular, can provide knowledge here. James Ladyman has defended scientism about metaphysics (thinking about existence), Daniel Dennett has championed scientism about understanding what goes on inside us (introspection), Sam Harris has argued for scientism about morality – we could go on and on.[24]

But others have gone much further. Bold versions of scientism say that only science provides knowledge in *all realms of life*, including all the above. That is also how the American philosopher of science and critic of scientism Massimo Pigliucci understands the term: scientism is "a totalizing attitude that regards science as the ultimate standard and arbiter of all interesting questions; or alternatively that seeks to expand the very definition and scope of science to encompass all aspects of human knowledge and understanding."[25] You might think that this must be a straw man of scientism. Surely nobody accepts so bold a view? However, several scientists and philosophers call themselves adherents of scientism in this sense and

[22] Francis Crick, *The Astonishing Hypothesis: The Scientific Search for the Soul* (New York: Touchstone, 1994), 3.

[23] Dick Swaab, *We Are Our Brains* (New York: Spiegel & Grau, 2014), 327, 328.

[24] See Don Ross, James Ladyman, and David Spurrett, "In Defence of Scientism," in James Ladyman, Don Ross, David Spurrett, and John Collier, *Every Thing Must Go: Metaphysics Naturalized* (Oxford: Oxford University Press, 2007), 1–65; Daniel Dennett, *Consciousness Explained* (London: Penguin, 1991); Sam Harris, *The Moral Landscape: How Science Can Determine Human Values* (New York: Free Press, 2010).

[25] Massimo Pigliucci, "New Atheism and the Scientistic Turn in the Atheism Movement," *Midwest Studies in Philosophy* 37, no. 1 (2013): 144.

explicitly embrace this view. For example, here is what the American philosopher Alex Rosenberg in defending scientism says about how he understands the term. Scientism is

> the conviction that the methods of science are the only reliable ways to secure knowledge of anything; that science's description of the world is correct in its fundamentals…. Science provides all the significant truths about reality, and knowing such truths is what real understanding is all about…. Being scientistic just means treating science as our exclusive guide to reality, to nature – both our own nature and everything else's.[26]

Unsurprisingly, Rosenberg also ends up defending atheism. In fact, the book in which he defends scientism is named *The Atheist's Guide to Reality*. Bolder versions of scientism and atheism are inextricably intertwined.

British chemist Peter Atkins is equally clear on the issue: "Science is the sole route to true, complete, and perfect knowledge."[27] He defends what he calls the "limitless power of science"[28] and in doing so claims that "scientists, with their implicit trust in reductionism, are privileged to be at the summit of knowledge, and to see further into truth than any of their contemporaries…. There is no reason to expect that science cannot deal with any aspect of existence."

In modest and bolder versions, scientism is rampant in contemporary intellectual culture: it is assumed and endorsed inside and outside academia by influential scientists and philosophers writing about evolutionary theory, genetics, morality, belief in God, brain science,

[26] Alex Rosenberg, *The Atheist's Guide to Reality: Enjoying Life without Illusions* (New York: W. W. Norton, 2011), 6–8. For a similar claim, see Peter W. Atkins, "Science as Truth," *History of the Human Sciences* 8, no. 2 (1995): 97–102.

[27] Peter W. Atkins, *Galileo's Finger: The Ten Great Ideas of Science* (Oxford: Oxford University Press, 2003), 237.

[28] Peter W. Atkins, "The Limitless Power of Science," in *Nature's Imagination: The Frontiers of Scientific Vision*, ed. John Cornwell (Oxford: Oxford University Press), 122–132.

psychology, and philosophy.[29] From there, scientism also wields influence on various social and professional practices, such as medicine, law, education, religion, and child-rearing. We need to take it seriously.

The Remarkable Success of Science and Its Applications

A good place to start in taking scientism seriously is to explore what can be said for it.[30] The first and rather obvious thing to note is that science has been tremendously successful. It has discovered many truths that we would not have unearthed without science. Sometimes, these truths are extremely complex and detailed. And they can be grand and unifying, giving us insight into a wide variety of phenomena. Evolutionary theory explains all biodiversity on earth, and the big bang theory the origin of the universe. Science makes seemingly wild and unlikely predictions that yet turn out to be true. Albert Einstein, for instance, was able to predict the bending of light by the gravity of the sun. This phenomenon was confirmed years later by an expedition witnessing a solar eclipse on May 29, 1919. The famous Higgs boson had been postulated for a long time, but it took years of extremely detailed research before this elementary particle was actually found. One paper on the Higgs boson has more than 5,000 authors – in fact, it has 9 pages describing the research and 24 pages listing all the authors. Science is hard work, and it has been spectacularly successful.

Alex Rosenberg takes such examples to count in favor of scientism: "The phenomenal accuracy of its prediction … and the breathtaking extent and detail of its explanations are powerful reasons to believe that physics is the whole truth about reality."[31]

---

[29] For a description of the influence of scientism, see Austin L. Hughes, "The Folly of Scientism," *The New Atlantis* 37 (2012): 32–50.

[30] I have addressed these and other reasons in more detail in my "Ten Reasons to Embrace Scientism."

[31] Rosenberg, *The Atheist's Guide to Reality*, 25.

It is easy to be deeply impressed with the predictions, detail, accuracy, and explanatory scope of science. Yet, it should be clear that it is a rather large leap from this all the way to the idea that "physics is the whole truth about reality." If you come across a book or a documentary or a program or whatever that is full of detailed knowledge, how would that give you any reason to think there is no truth beyond it? That science provides knowledge or at least often rational belief, then, is no reason to think that no knowledge is to be found elsewhere.

Something similar holds for the applications of science. Science has deeply affected our lives by radically changing transportation, medicine, agriculture, communication, and even the way we think of ourselves, our history, and our future. It is hard not to be impressed with the pervasiveness of science's applications in our society. Again, though, the fact that science has a wide range of implications doesn't mean that it has no limits or that only science provides knowledge.

But isn't there agreement or consensus or at least convergence toward consensus in science, whereas there is just vast disagreement on pretty much any topic beyond science? Take the COVID-19 measures, the existence of God (which God?), or international politics. You'll find almost as many views on these issues as there are people. But when it comes to the universal law of gravity, the law of conservation of mass, Dalton's law of partial pressures, Fourier's law of heat conduction, or Heisenberg's uncertainty principle, we find overwhelming agreement among scientists. Doesn't that give us reason to trust science and to distrust any other source that claims to provide knowledge?

I don't think it does. True, there are parts of science that pretty much all scientists agree on, such as the laws that I just mentioned. But there are also vast stretches of science that scientists disagree on: how life came about on earth, how quantum theory can be reconciled with general and special relativity, how the universe will end. Not only that, but there is also much beyond science that people agree on: the Netherlands is north of Spain (no science is needed to know that), killing for fun is morally wrong, no fully transparent object has a shadow, some people are shy whereas others are not – we could go on and on. Obviously, if you reject scientism, you don't thereby accept just any claim that is not scientific. There is much nonsense, bias, wishful thinking, lying, ignorance, irrationality, and stupidity beyond science. But then there is also much knowledge to be found outside of its boundaries. Such knowledge, I would suggest, is even compatible with disagreement. We know that female circumcision is wrong, that forced conversion is reprehensible, that burning widows is horrendous, that stoning after allegations of adultery is immoral. That some people on this planet disagree with us on these things is hardly a reason to reject our claim to knowledge. In fact, according to a widely embraced view in philosophy, it is perfectly possible for someone to disagree with others and still have knowledge.[32] Even more importantly, the whole issue applies to atheism itself. For the atheist claims to *know* that God doesn't exist, while billions of people disagree. Even the atheist, therefore, will have to accept that there can be knowledge in the face of disagreement.

Science Is Counterintuitive

Maybe the fact that much of science is counterintuitive gives us a reason to embrace scientism. Consider, for example, curved space-time or the bilocation of electrons. Don't such crazy but by now well-established scientific ideas show that we can't trust anything beyond science? According to the biologist Lewis Wolpert, for instance,

> both the ideas that science generates and the way in which science is carried out are entirely counter-intuitive and against common sense – by which I mean that scientific ideas cannot be acquired by

---

[32] See several of the essays in Richard Feldman and Ted A. Warfield, eds., *Disagreement* (Oxford: Oxford University Press, 2010).

simple inspection of phenomena and that they are very often out-side everyday experience.... I would almost contend that if some-thing fits with common sense it almost certainly isn't science.[33]

Alex Rosenberg would wholeheartedly agree:

Science – especially physics and biology – reveals that reality is com-pletely different from what most people think. It's not just different from what credulous religious believers think. Science reveals that reality is stranger than even many atheists recognize.[34]

One might think, then, that many scientific discoveries are so coun-terintuitive that we can no longer trust our intuitions or what we call common sense. We can only rely on science.

There is an important kernel of truth in this suggestion. Much of what science discovers on the macrolevel (the cosmos, black holes, and space-time) and the microlevel (the seemingly absurd behavior of electrons, in particular) differs radically from what we witness on the daily-life level. Electrons can have multiple locations. But cars, chairs, and shopping malls can't, nor can you or I – I wish I could. Space can be curved, but the space between you and your kitchen or between your home town and the nearest national park is never curved. In fact, it is hard to see how it could be curved. We should note, though, that this daily-life level (call it the mesolevel) is exactly what common sense is concerned with, as are visual perception, memory, and other sources of knowledge that we frequently use. All that follows from scientific discoveries that are counterintuitive

[33] Lewis Wolpert, *The Unnatural Nature of Science* (Cambridge, MA: Harvard University Press, 1992), 1, 11.

[34] Rosenberg, *The Atheist's Guide to Reality*, ix. See also Ross, Ladyman, and Spurrett, "In Defence of Scientism," 16–17: "Philosophers have often regarded as impossible states of affairs that science has come to entertain. For example, metaphysicians confidently pronounced that non-Euclidean geometry is impossible as a model of physical space, that it is impossible that there not be deterministic causation, that non-absolute time is impossible, and so on. Physicists learned to be comfortable with each of these ideas, along with others that confound the expectations of common sense more profoundly."

is that we should be careful not to make intuitive judgments on levels that are really different from the mesolevel.

But wait a second – what about God? Isn't God supposed to be omnipotent, perfectly good, eternal, omnipresent? That doesn't sound like a mesolevel. It seems more like a macrolevel *in excelsis*. Perhaps the counterintuitiveness of science doesn't plead against common sense, but doesn't it throw something of a shadow on belief in God? That's an interesting suggestion. But we should note that we have now moved far away from scientism to a specific objection to belief in God. Even if belief in God is somehow in trouble, it doesn't follow that scientism is true.

On classical theism, such as mainstream Christianity, God is not a very large material object, such as the universe. Of course, God is not like many mesolevel objects either, such as tables, chairs, trees, computers, and skateboards. God does resemble something we are familiar with, namely, a person. Persons have a will, knowledge, power, emotions, and intentions; they are beings that act and communicate. At the same time, though, God is thought to be radically different from the persons we are familiar with: God is bodiless, eternal, infinite in power and goodness. That science at the macro- and microlevel reveals much that is utterly counterintuitive doesn't seem to count against belief in God. But the fact that God is in so many ways utterly unlike the things we deal with in our daily lives raises legitimate worries about whether we can properly believe in God and whether we can actually know God. This is no reason to embrace scientism, but it is something to keep in the back of our minds until we return to arguments against belief in God.

Science as Debunker

Another interesting consideration for scientism is that science provides *evolutionary debunking arguments* for various commonsense beliefs, moral beliefs, and religious beliefs. The basic idea is that we hold these beliefs because they turned out to be evolutionarily advantageous – for instance, because they increased our chances of survival – and that this has nothing to do with their truth. American psychologist Jesse Bering, for example, has argued that people have religious beliefs, such as that God exists, that God has performed a miracle, or that God has listened to their prayers, because they have a Hyperactive Agency Detection Device (HADD). This mechanism detects agency – it tells us that a fast-moving shadow must be a running human or animal, that the rustling in the bushes means there is a large animal there, that these stones must have been stacked here by another person for some reason, and so on. Bering's point is that evolution has shaped the HADD in such a way that it is hyperactive: it will often also discern agency where there is none. In many people, it induces the belief that there is some kind of agency behind reality as a whole – a God. People with hyperactive agency detection are more likely to survive than those with normal agency detection. After all, if it is hyperactive, it will sometimes be mistaken, but it will also hardly ever miss important clues of agency. Maybe the sounds in the bushes are made by a crawling tiger, maybe not. You'd better be safe than sorry.[35]

American philosopher Sharon Street has argued that the shaping forces of our evolutionary history on our *moral* beliefs undermine belief in objective moral values.[36] Her argument is philosophical in nature: there may be objective moral values and truths out there, but if so, there's no reason to think that evolution tracks those truths. Let's contrast our moral beliefs with beliefs based on our senses. If you don't smell that the food is rotten, you may die from it, and if you don't see the canyon, you may fall into it. However, there's often no particular evolutionary advantage to believing moral truths. Evolution

---

[35] See Jesse Bering, *The God Instinct: The Psychology of Souls, Destiny, and the Meaning of Life* (London: Nicholas Brealey, 2011).

[36] See Sharon Street, "A Darwinian Dilemma for Realist Theories of Value," *Philosophical Studies* 127, no. 1 (2006): 109–166.

generally selects what is conducive to survival, such as group bonding, but there's no reason to think it has actually tracked moral reality. In fact, some behavior seems highly adaptive from an evolutionary point of view, yet it is utterly immoral; think, for instance, of a male gynecologist using his own sperm in fertility treatments – something that, unfortunately, isn't just a thought experiment.

These debunking arguments are clearly more interesting than the ones we've seen so far for scientism. Note, though, that each of them establishes a rather modest version of scientism, nothing remotely like the claim that only science provides knowledge in all realms of life. They are more restricted and, therefore, also much more plausible. They are confined to belief in gods or to belief in objective moral truths. Yet, a lot of work must still be done in order for arguments like these to succeed. First and foremost, they must truly *explain*, say, belief in God. That is easier said than done. Of course, one can construe an evolutionary just-so story that nicely explains why so many people believe in God. The problem is that *many* such stories can be construed. In order for such stories to be viable, we should not just tell them but operationalize them and thoroughly test them. The results should be systematically replicable. The field of the cognitive science of religion teems with rival explanations for belief in God, such as neurological explanations and explanations in terms of evolutionary advantage or evolutionary by-product. So far, there is no clear winner at all.

Not only should adherents of scientism establish a solid, robust, replicated theory that clearly trumps its rivals, but this theory should also be *debunking*. In other words, it should undermine the rationality of belief in God. But there is by now a whole array of philosophical arguments for the compatibility of neurological and evolutionary explanations for belief in God.[37] God, on mainstream religious traditions, uses countless neurological and biological processes, such

---

[37] For a helpful overview, see Hans Van Eyghen, *Arguing from Cognitive Science of Religion: Is Religious Belief Debunked?* (London: Bloomsbury, 2020).

as people perceiving their environment and remembering things, to bring about certain purposes. It isn't clear why God couldn't, in a similar fashion, use a natural process, like an evolutionary one, to bring about belief in him.[38] In order to make progress here, the friend of scientism will have to meet these two challenges.

There are further domains in which we find debunking arguments. We should think especially of beliefs about free will and beliefs about acting for reasons. Some experiments, for instance, have been taken to show that the brain prepares free actions well before we are consciously aware of the intention to execute them. Particularly well-known are American neuroscientist Benjamin Libet's experiments on free will. These studies showed that brain activity having to do with a particular action occurred *before* subjects reported any awareness of a conscious decision to perform that act. This has been referred to as our *readiness potential*. It has been claimed on the basis of such experiments that free will doesn't exist and that we need to revise our concept of moral responsibility.[39] After all, don't these experiments suggest that the true initiators of our volitional acts are unconscious brain processes rather than decisions of our alleged free will? In addition, some studies on decision-making allegedly demonstrate that the explanations we provide for our actions are in fact post hoc rationalizations, because our actions actually stem from causes of which we are completely unaware.[40] If you make sure that people find a 10-dollar bill before they walk out on the streets, they're much more likely to help a stranger in need, but nobody would cite the 10-dollar bill as an

[38] See, for instance, Justin M. Barrett, *Born Believers: The Science of Children's Religious Belief* (New York: Free Press, 2012) for a discussion on whether or not contemporary evolutionary explanations of religious beliefs are truly debunking.

[39] See Benjamin Libet, "Unconscious Cerebral Initiative and the Role of Conscious Will in Voluntary Action," *Behavioral and Brain Sciences* 8 (1985): 529–566; Derk Pereboom, *Living without Free Will* (Cambridge: Cambridge University Press, 2001).

[40] See, for instance, Daniel Wegner, *The Illusion of Conscious Will* (Cambridge, MA: MIT Press, 2002).

explanation for their behavior, even though it is. From among all possible pairs of shoes, people are highly likely to select the pair situated in the upper right corner, even if all the other pairs of shoes are identical. Yet, nobody cites the location of the shoes as an explanation for why they selected that particular pair, although it apparently is. And so on. The idea here, then, is that science provides not just what philosophers call an *undercutting* defeater, which would show that the belief is not rational, but also a *rebutting* defeater: science shows that these beliefs are false or illusory. We don't really know the reasons why we act at all, and free will is an illusion. However, both these experiments and their ramifications are highly contested. Libet himself, for instance, rejected the idea that his experiments showed there is no free will. Others have argued that the concept of free will that underlies these arguments is mistaken.

This suggests that bold scientism is unwarranted, but that more-modest versions of scientism applying only to a particular domain of life may be more promising. But in order for modest versions of scientism to be truly plausible, we need more-solid experiments and philosophical reasoning that actually shows how these experiments undercut people's ordinary beliefs in these domains.

Is Scientism Self-Refuting?

The arguments for scientism need more work in order to be convincing, then. But can we, perhaps, also positively show that scientism is problematic?[41] Various philosophers have argued that this

---

[41] Two of the three arguments I lay out here are ones that I've explored myself in more detail elsewhere. See my "The Fundamental Argument against Scientism," in *Science Unlimited? The Challenges of Scientism*, ed. Maarten Boudry and Massimo Pigliucci (Chicago: Chicago University Press, 2018), 165–184, and my "Should We Accept Scientism? The Argument from Self-Referential Incoherence," in *What Is Scientific Knowledge? An Introduction to Contemporary Epistemology of Science*, ed. Kevin McCain and Kostas Kampourakis (New York: Routledge, 2019), 274–287.

is indeed the case. A good starting point here is considering how scientism bears on itself. As Jeroen de Ridder points out:

> Scientism suffers from self-referential problems. Not being a scientific claim itself, it would seem scientism cannot be known by anyone. This raises the question of why anyone should assert or believe it in the first place.[42]

The Swedish philosopher Mikael Stenmark makes a similar point:

> What we want to know is whether science sets the limits for reality. The problem is that since we can only obtain knowledge about reality by means of scientific methods ..., we must use those methods whose scope is in question to determine the scope of these very same methods. If we used *non*-scientific methods we could never come to *know* the answer to our question, because there is according to scientistic faith no knowledge outside science. We are therefore forced to admit either that we cannot avoid arguing in a circle or that the acceptance of [scientism] is a matter of superstition or blind faith.[43]

The first step of the argument is that friends of scientism are committed to the view that they *know* that scientism is true. This seems quite plausible. After all, adherents of scientism won't claim they believe in it just because they like it. They'll take it that it is perfectly rational to accept it and not arbitrary. The second step is that we can't know that scientism is true on the basis of scientific research. For scientism is not some empirical truth that we can find out by way of setting up an experiment or doing statistical research. Nor does it seem to be an a priori truth that can be deduced by mathematical or logical methods from elementary truths that we know a priori. Rather, it seems to be a principle that needs to be backed up

---

[42] De Ridder, "Science and Scientism in Popular Science Writing," 27.
[43] See Mikael Stenmark, *Scientism: Science, Ethics and Religion* (New York: Routledge, 2018), 22–23.

by philosophical argumentation. And whatever philosophy is, it is widely considered not to be one of the sciences.

I find this argument promising. In fact, arguments from self-referential incoherence – as philosophers call them – have a venerable pedigree. Already in the *Theaetetus*, Socrates uses an argument from self-referential incoherence against Protagoras's claim that man is the measure of all things.[44] Even if we update the claim by saying that humans rather than just men are the measure of all things, it still faces the same problem. If it's true, then in thinking it's false, one must be right – because humans are the measure of all things. And in fact, many people think it's false. Therefore, if it's true, it must be false.

The argument also showed up in criticisms of logical positivism. Logical positivism was an early twentieth-century movement that was meant to make scientific inquiry more rigorous. It boldly asserted that any claim that cannot be empirically verified and that is not analytic either (i.e., not a tautology) is literally meaningless. Some logical positivists, such as Alfred Ayer, Rudolf Carnap, Moritz Schlick, and Otto Neurath, then made an important discovery. They found that this bold assertion didn't meet its own criterion. The verification criterion, as it came to be called, could not itself be empirically verified, and it wasn't an analytic truth either. So, they simply abandoned the criterion. Nowadays, the argument from self-referential incoherence is sometimes used to counter the postmodernist claim that everything is relative: if that claim is true, then it is itself only relatively true and, therefore, cannot be categorically accepted. Thus, the argument has a long and fruitful tradition in philosophy.

According to British chemist Peter Atkins, there are no boundaries to the competence of science.[45] But if this first consideration

---

[44] See Plato, *Theaetetus*, trans. M. J. Levett (Glasgow: University of Glasgow Press, 1977), 57–58, 171a–c.

[45] See Atkins, "Science as Truth," 97.

against scientism is sound, there is probably at least one boundary to the competence of science. Science is incompetent to motivate bold scientism, that is, to provide sufficient scientific support to make belief in scientism rational. This is, of course, not a problem for science. All things in life have boundaries. The reasonable thing to do would be to stick to science but to abandon scientism.

Science is Based on Common Sense

Another serious worry for scientism is that science itself seems based on common sense and other nonscientific belief sources. In other words, if you reject common sense, you'll have to reject science as well. We find a short formulation of the argument in the writings of the British ethicist Mary Midgley:

> Science cannot stand alone. We cannot believe its propositions without first believing in a great many other … things, such as the existence of the external world, the reliability of our senses, memory and informants, and the validity of logic. If we do believe in these things, we already have a world far wider than that of science.[46]

And we find another brief characterization of this argument in an article by the Dutch philosopher René van Woudenberg. Scientists may

> bite the bullet and deny that extra-scientific beliefs ever amount to knowledge. This, however, would be deeply problematic. For scientific knowledge depends in many ways on extra-scientific knowledge, for instance, on what we know through perception, such as that the thermometer now reads 118 degrees Fahrenheit. Without

---

[46] Mary Midgley, *Science as Salvation: A Modern Myth and Its Meaning* (London: Routledge, 1992), 108.

such extra-scientific knowledge it is hard to see how science could even get started.[47]

Thus, in order for science to even get started, our commonsense beliefs, like our memory beliefs, beliefs based on visual perception, metaphysical beliefs on a daily-life level, and, according to some, even our beliefs based on introspection,[48] must usually be reliable. If you remove the foundation of science because it is nonscientific, the building of science collapses. If you keep the foundation, even though it is nonscientific, then why would you reject other nonscientific sources of belief?

This applies not just to the personal beliefs and experiences of the scientist, such as what she believes on the basis of what she sees and smells, what she remembers, or what she deduces. It also applies to the principles that, though constitutive of science, are not themselves based on science. I mean the general principles that make science work. Take the criteria for theory selection. These are the various positive properties that a scientist considers when she compares rival hypotheses and rival theories. Among them are explanatory scope (how much do they explain?), explanatory power (how well do they explain?), predictive power (how much and how well do they predict?), coherence with background knowledge, internal consistency, simplicity, and elegance. In comparing several theories, the scientist will have to compare their relative weight and balance them, because often, one theory does better on one criterion and another theory on another criterion. We can also think of principles like the knowability of the world or the uniformity of nature. All such principles are constitutive of science, but they are

---

[47] See René van Woudenberg, "Limits of Science and the Christian Faith," *Perspectives on Science and Christian Faith* 65, no. 1 (2013): 26. See also René van Woudenberg, "Truths That Science Cannot Touch," *Philosophia Reformata* 76, no. 2 (2011): 169–186.

[48] See many of the contributions in Anthony I. Jack and Andreas Roepstorff, eds., "Trusting the Subject? The Use of Introspective Evidence in Cognitive Science," vol. 1, special issue, *Journal of Consciousness Studies* 10, no. 9–10 (2003).

not themselves based on science. Science can only start from them; it cannot prove them in any way. That seems to be another limit: the basis of science cannot be known on the basis of science.

Scientific Knowledge as the Best

Maybe, though, there is an alternative route. Perhaps bold scientism is too strong and modest scientism too weak, at least as things stand. Something like a middle road has been trodden by the American philosopher Moti Mizrahi. He defines scientism as the view that "of all the knowledge we have, scientific knowledge is the *best* knowledge."[49] Clearly, this view is radically different from bold scientism, which, after all, denies knowledge outside of the sciences. Mizrahi's scientism, however, is perfectly compatible with the idea that some people have religious knowledge by way of experience and revelation. It's also compatible with the suggestion that we can have moral knowledge by intuition or by commonsense reasoning. Scientific knowledge is just better.

Straightaway, then, scientism would lose much of its bite. But even apart from that, there are substantial worries about this alternative construal of scientism. For example, in what sense is science supposed to provide the best knowledge? Is scientific knowledge better than my nonscientific knowledge that the earth is made of matter, that I exist, or that $2 + 5 = 7$? That seems wildly implausible. Scientific knowledge is often much more provisional than such commonsense knowledge.

The claim seems implausible, then, for knowledge from common sense. What about the humanities, such as history, linguistics, ethics, and philosophy more generally? Mizrahi points out that scientific publications are much more numerous and often have a higher

---

[49] Moti Mizrahi, "What's So Bad about Scientism?," *Social Epistemology* 31, no. 4 (2017): 351–367.

impact than publications in the humanities. That is true, but that may well be because a great deal more money goes into the sciences, given the practical applications they usually have. Mizrahi also claims that scientific knowledge is qualitatively better in that it has more explanatory power, instrumental success, and predictive power. This seems right for many sciences and many disciplines in the humanities – although some disciplines in the humanities, such as linguistics, have tremendous explanatory power and great instrumental success. Yet, what follows? The humanities are concerned with really challenging objects, such as moral goodness and badness, or the distant past. It may well be in the very nature of the humanities that knowledge of these objects is more difficult to obtain than scientific knowledge. So what? If this does not prevent the humanities from generating knowledge, it looks like scientism has become a somewhat trivial and uninteresting claim. In summary, Mizrahi's alternative lends little support to atheism and is not particularly attractive.[50]

Fundamentalism

If scientism is plagued by all these problems, how come quite a few atheists have bought into it? You really don't need scientism to become an atheist or to defend atheism. I think an interesting explanation is that scientism may be a variety of fundamentalism. After all, scientism provides certainty in an uncertain world; it gives us a narrative that helps us make sense of things.[51]

---

[50] That science is only the *best* way to acquire knowledge was recently also argued by six Finnish scholars: see Johan Hietanen, Petri Turunen, Ilmari Hirvonen, Janne Karisto, Ilkka Pättiniemi, and Henrik Saarinen, "How *Not* to Criticise Scientism," *Metaphilosophy* 51, no. 4 (2020): 522–547. Their version of scientism acknowledges that the humanities, the arts, the social sciences, and common sense deliver knowledge as well.

[51] This has also been suggested by George F. R. Ellis. I provide a firmer background in the literature on fundamentalism, though. What I say here is based on my "Scientism

But isn't it offensive – or at least highly pejorative – to qualify scientism as fundamentalism? In using this term, don't we tacitly imply that adherents of scientism are dogmatic, estranged from real life, unwilling to have an open-minded conversation? I agree that the word *fundamentalism* often has such connotations in common parlance. However, in academic situations, it tends to be used in a more neutral fashion. We will see that it pays off to interpret scientism as fundamentalism: it makes us better understand what is going on. So, let me explain how I use the term.

As American historian George Marsden and others have shown in detail,[52] the origins of the term *fundamentalism* can be clearly identified. It was first used to describe various conservative and somewhat strident Protestant movements in the early twentieth century in the United Kingdom and the United States. They considered certain modern developments a threat to their faith, things such as evolutionary theory, liberal ethics, and historical-biblical criticism. Consequently, they formulated what they considered to be indubitable truths, so-called *fundamentals*. Among those fundamental, indubitable truths were the divinity of Christ, the inerrancy of the holy scriptures, and Christ's substitutionary atonement. These fundamentals were laid out in detail in a collection of essays published in 1917, *The Fundamentals: A Testimony to the Truth*.

Some scholars, such as the Scottish university educator Ninian Smart,[53] have suggested that we should stick to this rather narrow understanding of fundamentalism. However, most scholars have gone on to identify several other religious movements as fundamentalist,

and Fundamentalism: What Science Can Learn from Mainstream Religions." For comparison, see George F. R. Ellis, "Fundamentalism in Science, Theology, and the Academy," in *Human Identity at the Intersection of Science, Technology, and Religion*, ed. Nancey Murphy and Christopher C. Knight (London: Routledge, 2010), 57–76.

[52] George M. Marsden, *Fundamentalism and American Culture: The Shaping of Twentieth-Century Evangelicalism, 1870–1925* (Oxford: Oxford University Press, 1980); *Understanding Fundamentalism and Evangelicalism* (Grand Rapids: Eerdmans, 1991).

[53] Ninian Smart, *The World's Religions*, 2nd ed. (Cambridge: Cambridge University Press, 1998).

such as Haredi Judaism, some kinds of Salafism and Wahhabism, and branches of TULIP Calvinism. Various movements that are a blend of religion and nationalism are often also included, such as the political movement Rashtriya Swayamsevak Sangh in Hinduism.[54] In fact, the list has become even longer because certain kinds of secular fundamentalisms are now included – for example, neo-Nazism, radical environmentalism, communism, feminist fundamentalism, gender fundamentalism, and pedagogical fundamentalism. So, what are the boundaries of the concept, and is there a principled way of using the term?

I think there is. Over the last two decades or so, a number of authors have suggested that we should treat fundamentalism as a family resemblance concept.[55] The idea of a family resemblance was first formulated by the famous Austrian-British philosopher Ludwig Wittgenstein.[56] His idea is that some things have no hard, necessary, or sufficient conditions. Rather, they are constituted by stereotypical characteristics. Take games, says Wittgenstein. There is no characteristic that all games have in common. Some games, such as tennis, have a complicated set of rules, but others don't – for instance, trying to throw the ball as high as you can. Some games are competitive, but other games are not. Some are meant for entertainment, others not (they are merely for training). Games just share similarities with other games. Something is a game if it has enough of those characteristics; it doesn't need to have all of them. Things are similar for the various kinds of fundamentalism: they have certain characteristics, but they don't need to have all of them.

---

[54] See Martin E. Marty and R. Scott Appleby, eds., *The Fundamentalism Project*, 5 vols. (Chicago: University of Chicago Press, 1991–1995).

[55] See Gabriel A. Almond, R. Scott Appleby, and Emmanuel Sivan, *Strong Religion: The Rise of Fundamentalisms around the World* (Chicago: University of Chicago Press, 2003); Malise Ruthven, *Fundamentalism: The Search for Meaning* (Oxford: Oxford University Press, 2004).

[56] See Ludwig Wittgenstein, *Philosophical Investigations* (Oxford: Blackwell, 2001).

So, what are those characteristics? I think there are three collections of characteristics.[57] The first concerns the fact that fundamentalists are reactionary: rather than being a freestanding, sovereign movement, they respond to modern developments they consider to be threatening. Among such developments are liberal ethics (for example, the propagation of the rights of homosexuals), scientific developments in evolutionary biology and cosmology, and individualism. Fundamentalisms, therefore, are time-indexed: they respond to modern developments, particularly those occurring since the early twentieth century.

The second collection of characteristics have to do with the fact that, paradoxically, fundamentalist movements are themselves highly modern: they seek certainty and control in an uncertain world.[58] They do so by ascribing a particular status – for example, being literally and historically inerrant and infallible – to such holy scriptures as the Qur'an, the Sharia, the Old and New Testaments, the Halacha, the Talmud, or the Guru Granth Sahib. They are also highly modern in employing particularly modern ends – public debates, the internet, social media – to reach people with their message.

The final collection of characteristics has to do with the fact that fundamentalisms embrace a grand, overarching narrative about the world. Often, the basic idea is that there once was a paradisaical state, that this state was lost due to human fault, and that we now need to restore the original and perfect state. Humans, then, have a special place in this world picture. Another part of the story is some kind of cosmic moral dualism, sometimes called Manicheism, named after the dualistic Gnostic religious system of the third-century Persian thinker Manes. Here, the idea is that good and evil are the only two forces in the world,

---

[57] What follows is based on a scoping review that I carried out with others; see Nora Kindermann, Rik Peels, Anke I. Liefbroer, and Linda Schoonmade, "Mapping Definitions of 'Fundamentalism': A Scoping Review" (unpublished manuscript, February 16, 2023).

[58] J. S. Krüger, "Religious Fundamentalism: Aspects of a Comparative Framework of Understanding," *Verbum et Ecclesia* 27, no. 3 (2006): 886–908.

that they are constantly at war, and that every human being is either on the good side or on the bad side – there is nothing in-between.

Saying that fundamentalism is a family resemblance concept means that none of these characteristics are necessary for fundamentalism. Nor are they sufficient. Thus, one can embrace cosmic dualism without being a fundamentalist. And one can be a fundamentalist even if one does not believe that there once was a perfect, paradisaical state. A movement only has to have *enough of* these characteristics. Paradigm cases of fundamentalism have all or most characteristics; boundary cases have only some of them.

Note that being violent or having a disposition toward violence is not one of the stereotypical properties of fundamentalism. Obviously, some fundamentalists are violent. But that is usually because they are *also* extremists or even terrorists. Millions of Muslims, conservative Protestants, and so on, are fundamentalist without being violent toward others. They may do some *othering* – that is, they may regard outgroup members as deficient in certain ways. But such othering is quite different from employing violence.

Before we move on, let me also note that fundamentalism is not just a set of beliefs or a belief system.[59] Of course, fundamentalisms come with beliefs, but they also come with emotions (for instance, anger or grievances), hopes and desires, actions, and practical things such as symbols, rituals, and objects.

Is Scientism Fundamentalist?

In the past, I've been hesitant to describe scientism as a variety of fundamentalism. Scientism just seems so different from, say, fundamentalist Protestant Evangelicalism. For one thing,

---

[59] Contrary to what is suggested by Wynette Barton, "What's Fundamental about Fundamentalism?," *Psychological Perspectives* 52, no. 4 (2009): 439; Michael Baurmann, "Rational Fundamentalism? An Explanatory Model of Fundamentalist Beliefs," *Episteme* 4, no. 2 (2007): 157.

fundamentalist Protestant Evangelicals reject crucial scientific developments, whereas adherents of scientism celebrate them. However, since I've been delving more deeply into family resemblance analyses of fundamentalism and of specific religious and secular fundamentalist movements, I've changed my mind on this. I now believe that scientism can rightly be regarded as a variety of secular fundamentalism. It may not be a paradigm case of fundamentalism, but it clearly has many of the characteristics of fundamentalism – enough to count as a variety of fundamentalism. And seeing this will help us to better understand scientism.

Scientism is undoubtedly a reactionary movement. It responds to various societal developments that it considers dangerous or harmful, both intellectually and morally. Here, we can think especially of the societal influence of the major religions, including Christianity and Islam. We can also think of particularly modern phenomena, such as the spread of conservative Islam in the West, which is partly due to migration. We can think of anthroposophy and other science-skeptical movements that have come to flourish in the twentieth century. In the United States, an important event that elicited scientistic response was the rise of the intelligent-design movement, which sought public recognition and desired space for intelligent design to be taught in high schools.

Scientism is also itself a particularly modern development. It seeks certainty in an uncertain and constantly changing world, and it claims that the only achievable certainty is to be had by way of scientific inquiry. No other source can be an intellectual guide in this world. Clearly, adherents of scientism have actively used modern media to reach their audiences: public debates, social media, lectures on YouTube, and podcasts. Obviously, scientism does not consider certain holy scriptures as infallible. But it clearly regards scientific writings, scientific methods, and scientific beliefs as the very best we have. An autobiography by Richard Dawkins is tellingly titled *Brief Candle in the Dark: My Life in Science*, and the cosmologist Carl Sagan uses the same metaphor in the title of his book *The Demon-Haunted World: Science as a Candle in the Dark* – this says it all.

Finally, scientism clearly provides a fundamentalist overarching narrative. The main difference with many other fundamentalist stories is that in this story, there never was a paradisaical state. Humans have been in the dark from the very beginning. At most, the darkness was deepened by things like institutional religion. Redemption is to be had by intellectual enlightenment, and that is to be found in the sciences. Only these can break the spell of religion, commonsense morality, and such illusions as those of free will and consciousness. Scientism also comes with Manicheism, or, as I'd prefer to call it, moral dualism. On the one hand, there are the blind and evil forces of religion, folk stupidity, tradition, and other sources that impede intellectual flourishing. On the other hand, there is the torch of scientific reason, which can enlighten us if we use it rightly.

Interpreting scientism as a variety of fundamentalism helps us better understand why someone would champion it. Adherents of scientism are usually fed up with the wishful thinking, naivete, pseudoscience, and dogmatism of some religious movements (often themselves fundamentalist), anthroposophists, and other science skeptics – and understandably so. In times of uncertainty, extremism, terrorism, and social polarization, they seek certainty and control and, therefore, reach for an instrument that has been particularly successful: science. They absolutize it, at the cost of all the knowledge, wisdom, beauty, and goodness that is to be found outside of science, particularly in religions. They come to see the world in dualistic terms: there are those who follow the torch of reason and those who reject it and lead humanity into darkness. I find this understandable but misguided: our world, its problems, and the solutions to these problems are all far more complex than that.

What Science Can Learn from Mainstream Religions

Religions have had to deal with extremist, fanaticist, and even terrorist movements for centuries. Ever since the birth of fundamentalism in the early twentieth century, religions have also had to counter fundamentalisms. Maybe scientists, scientific institutions, and journalists can learn something from religions in terms of how to deal with the scientific fundamentalism that we find in scientism.

First of all, mainstream religions have wisely opted not to meddle in scientific affairs. Religion is not about finding out scientific truths. We can leave that to the scientists. In fact, mainstream religions have lauded the scientific endeavor and gladly welcomed its tremendous achievements.

Similarly, scientists and scientific institutions should encourage scientists to stick to their expertise. As an expert in evolutionary biology, it is perfectly fine for Richard Dawkins to inform the larger public on various biological issues, as he does in some of his more public books – for example, *The Greatest Show on Earth*, which presents the evidence for evolutionary theory. It is *not* fine for him to elaborate on the moral and social effects of religion, explanations of why people are religious, or the tenability of various God conceptions. That is, unless he deeply delves into all the literature that is required for being an expert in these fields; for instance, the sociological literature on the societal effects of religion, studies in the cognitive science of religion, and systematic-theological work on the doctrine of God, anthropology, and the theory of revelation.

Also, many mainstream religions have learned to live with a lot of uncertainty. They consider the Old and New Testaments, the Halacha, the Talmud, or the Guru Granth Sahib as divinely inspired holy scriptures. In many cases, they believe them to be more holy and more divinely inspired than the writings found in other religions. Yet, mainstream religions do *not* assert that these holy scriptures are *literally*, entirely *historically*, and *infallibly* true. They have resisted the modern urge to seek and find certainty and control in an uncertain and scary world by conferring an inerrant status to these texts. Rather, they suggest that God's word can be found in these writings and that that requires interpretation. Being a person of faith, then, is a matter of having hope, trust, commitment, belief, maybe even rational belief and knowledge – it does not require one to be *certain*.

Similarly, science and scientific institutions should not seek certainty or infallibility in science. Science gives us knowledge, as do many other sources, such as common sense, tradition, wisdom, and maybe even holy scriptures. Science should propagate and cultivate systematic doubt rather than certainty, as the American sociologist Robert K. Merton already argued.

Some scientists frequently say such things as "Everything is a matter of random mutation and natural selection," "We are our brains," "Matter is all there is," and "All our ideas are just social constructions." I understand why it can be helpful within particular disciplines to adopt such a reductionistic stance every now and then. For instance, one can study the brain in a neuroscientific way, but not the soul. Unsurprisingly, neuroscientists have a tendency to treat the human mind and human soul as if they are reducible to the brain. But there is no reason to think that that follows from the science itself. There is a wide variety of belief sources that provide knowledge, and science is only one of them. There are vast territories of actual and potential knowledge beyond science. We should remind ourselves of this and respect the boundaries of each academic discipline.

Many mainstream religions have learned to some extent to tolerate fundamentalist movements rather than expel them and to keep the conversation with them going rather than simply avoid them. Of course, fundamentalist movements often split from mainstream denominations and shut off the conversation themselves, partly by othering members of the mainstream religion. But leaders of, say, the Roman Catholic Church or the Anglican Communion have learned to keep talking to those who reject the wider church's policy, for instance, for being too liberal, for pursuing equal rights for men and women, or for seeking a nuanced hermeneutics of holy scriptures.

Similarly, science and scientific institutions should not reject or fire adherents of scientism nor shut off the conversation with them. Rather, they should continue to work with them and embrace their serious scientific work while continuously keeping a critical conversation going about their scientism – about its philosophical tenability, about its evidential underpinning, and about its harmful effects for science and society.

In response to fundamentalist movements, mainstream religions have upheld other sources of knowledge beyond their own religion and alleged revelation. Christianity and Judaism, for instance, have most of the time been fertile soil for rigorous academic thinking. I already mentioned the ideas that God has created the natural world in an orderly fashion and that humans have been created *imago Dei* (in the image of God), so that they are properly equipped to investigate and understand the world. But there's more. There's also the idea that humans are fallen and fallible; the idea is even that we suffer from original sin. We are therefore susceptible to self-deception, misperception, jumping to conclusions, and so on. Science can be a systematic endeavor to partly make good on this.[60] In Luke 10:27, Christians are called to love God with all their minds. Contrast this picture with, say, Hinduism, which teaches that the everyday world of material objects is an illusion (*maya*), or some polytheistic religions that see reality as a battleground for opposed divine forces, resulting in chaos. This is not to say that Hindus or polytheists can't do science – of course they can, and of course they do. But historically speaking,

---

[60] This has been extensively historically documented. See Peter Harrison, *The Fall of Man and the Foundations of Science* (Cambridge: Cambridge University Press, 2007).

Judaism and Christianity have provided an especially fruitful background, partly for theological reasons.

As a result, mainstream Christianity – mainstream Protestantism, Roman Catholicism, and the Orthodox Church – has always emphasized the value of serious academic scholarship, even if such scholarship seemed to conflict at some level with religious truths, as was the case for cosmology and evolutionary theory. Rather than straight-out rejecting these branches of science, as fundamentalisms did, these Christians developed various models showing how the two can go well together.

Similarly, science should acknowledge sources of knowledge beyond science. Naturally, it is not primarily concerned with those sources, unless as objects of academic inquiry. It is *science*, after all, not journalism or religion. Still, science should not discard these sources. While confirming the value of science, it should also acknowledge its limitations and thereby avoid scientism.

Atheism and Its Cognitive Frameworks

Evidentialism, distantionism, and scientism are influential frameworks. They aren't really motivations or arguments for atheism. Rather, they are ways of thinking or cognitive paradigms within which some people operate. Once someone works within such a paradigm, atheism becomes likely and in some cases even inevitable. What a public debate requires in such cases is not a criticism of atheistic arguments, let alone a series of arguments for belief in God, but a serious evaluation of that cognitive framework.

There are more frameworks conducive to atheism than the ones we've explored here. There's naturalism, materialism, physicalism, determinism, and reductionism, to mention only a few. These frameworks, however, are in fact often motivated by scientism. After all, materialists, physicalists, reductionists, and the like nowadays usually take it that science provides the evidence for these frameworks. So, if scientism is in trouble, this will cast a dark shadow on these other ways of thinking.

Out of the three cognitive frameworks we've explored in this chapter, scientism is undoubtedly the most influential and appealing in our times. Yet, the claims that only science provides knowledge, that science can answer all questions, and that science is our only guide to reality are really not backed up by science. There's nothing wrong with science, but such grand assertions should be rejected, not only because they are harmful to society and science itself but also because they don't hold water. Scientism can work at most in specific areas of life, such as free will, morality, belief in God, acting for reasons, or metaphysical intuition. Whether it does will depend on the quality of the arguments provided in that realm. So far, however, things don't look good for scientism. Scholars in different fields are needed to show whether or not the modest versions of scientism are mistaken. In order to evaluate claims about religious beliefs and experiences, we need theologians. In order to assess the logical validity and assumptions of scientistic arguments, we need philosophers. And in order to weigh the empirical evidence and judge the extent to which the hypotheses meet the criteria for good scientific-theory selection, we need scientists.

Our discussion of scientism gave us reason to think that metaphysical beliefs and beliefs from the senses, memory, and logical reasoning are all needed for doing science. It seems perfectly reasonable to adopt such beliefs, then, unless one can show that there's something wrong with them. Thus, our perceptual and common-sense beliefs are innocent until proven guilty rather than guilty until proven innocent.[61]

---

[61] Here, I follow the Scottish philosopher Thomas Reid. See, for instance, Thomas Reid, *An Inquiry into the Human Mind on the Principles of Common Sense*, ed. Derek R. Brookes (Edinburgh: Edinburgh University Press, 1997).

There are clear limits to science. To deny this is to turn science into some kind of "scientific imperialism," as John Dupré calls it.[62] Some of the limits concern science itself: it cannot discard its foundations in common sense, it cannot work without unscientific principles like criteria for theory selection, and it cannot do without fields in ethics like research integrity. But the boundaries also have to do with the infinitely large domain beyond science. As things stand, science gives us no substantial knowledge of history, the arts, moral truths, truths about God, introspective truths, and basic metaphysical truths, including those that are constitutive of science.[63] It gives us no wisdom; it doesn't provide aesthetic insight. In all these realms, we need other things than science to make progress: the humanities, common sense, moral intuition and moral reasoning, religious experience, the connoisseurship of art experts, and writers like Fyodor Dostoyevsky, Virginia Woolf, and Shūsaku Endō.

We should remain open-minded, though, toward the possibility that science undermines some of our commonsense beliefs in these realms or that it does provide knowledge on these issues – not only for the sake of that knowledge itself but also for the sake of better understanding atheism.

---

[62] See John Dupré, *Human Nature and the Limits of Science* (New York: Oxford University Press, 2002).

[63] Thus also Nicholas Rescher, *The Limits of Science* (Berkeley: University of California Press, 1984).

4 | The Presumption of Atheism

The Question

We've looked at motivations for atheism and atheistic frameworks. But there's another option in defending atheism that is available to the atheist: he may suggest that the onus of proof is on the theist. After all, the theist believes that there is a God, so it's up to the theist to show that there is a God. Anthony Flew famously dubbed this situation the "presumption of atheism."[1] But other atheists, such as John Mackie, adopt a different position: they say the onus of proof is equally on both sides. The theist believes that there is a God, so she should explain why; the atheist believes that there is no God, so he should explain why.[2]

Who is right? I think we can make progress by comparing the whole idea of a presumption of atheism with a contemporary movement in the philosophy of religion named *Reformed epistemology*. According to adherents of Reformed epistemology, belief

---

[1] Other atheists have taken the same stance, people such as Sam Harris, Aaron Holland, Michael Martin, Michael Scriven, and Michael Tooley. See Antony Flew, *The Presumption of Atheism and Other Philosophical Essays on God, Freedom and Immortality* (London: Elek/Pemberton, 1976); Sam Harris, *Letter to a Christian Nation* (London: Bantam, 2007), 6; Aaron Holland, "Consistency in Presuming Agnosticism," *Philo* 4, no. 1 (2001): 82–89; Michael Martin, *Atheism: A Philosophical Justification* (Philadelphia: Temple University Press, 1990); Michael Scriven, *Primary Philosophy* (New York: McGraw-Hill, 1966), 102–107; Michael Tooley, "Does God Exist?," in Alvin Plantinga and Michael Tooley, *Knowledge of God* (Oxford: Blackwell, 2008), 90–92.

[2] See John L. Mackie, *The Miracle of Theism: Arguments for and against the Existence of God* (Oxford: Clarendon, 1982), 8.

in God can be rational even if the believer has no arguments for God's existence. Just to be clear: that's perfectly compatible with the view that there *are* good arguments for God's existence, such as the cosmological argument, the fine-tuning argument, the moral argument, and the argument from consciousness.[3] The point of Reformed epistemology is that the religious believer does not *need* to have such arguments. Her belief in God can be entirely rational even if she cannot provide such arguments.

Reformed epistemology goes back to the theology of figures like Thomas Aquinas and John Calvin. Nowadays, it's championed with much philosophical acumen by such Christian philosophers as William Alston, Alvin Plantinga, and Nicholas Wolterstorff.[4] The basic idea of Reformed epistemology is that if God exists, it is not at all unlikely that he has made us in such a way that we can know that he exists without any sort of complex argumentation.

Could the atheist claim something similar? Obviously, he would not appeal to God, but he may well suggest that one doesn't really need any sort of complex arguments to know that God does not exist. The horrible suffering of many human beings and experiences of the emptiness of the universe, the chaos of everyday life, and the meaningless of much of what happens on our planet could, perhaps, suffice to justify atheism. This would square well with what we have seen so far in this book: atheists are often not primarily motivated by arguments but by experiences, ideals, and desires. If atheism can be justified by these things without any arguments,

[3] See Stefan Paas and Rik Peels, *God bewijzen: Argumenten voor en tegen geloven* [Why it's OK to believe in God] (Amsterdam: Balans, 2013).

[4] See William P. Alston, *Perceiving God: The Epistemology of Religious Experience* (Ithaca: Cornell University Press, 1991); Alvin Plantinga, *Warranted Christian Belief* (New York: Oxford University Press, 2000); Nicholas Wolterstorff, "Can Belief in God Be Rational If It Has No Foundations?," in *Faith and Rationality: Reason and Belief in God*, ed. Alvin Plantinga and Nicholas Wolterstorff (Notre Dame: University of Notre Dame Press, 1983), 135–186.

then some of the motivations for atheism that we encountered may provide perfectly proper justifications for atheism.[5]

A Dose of Epistemology

In order to see how the presumption of atheism would work, I will quickly take you through some basic concepts in epistemology. An important distinction is that between *basic* beliefs and *nonbasic* beliefs. Basic beliefs are not based on any arguments, while nonbasic beliefs are. For example, my belief that I had yogurt with raspberries for breakfast this morning is basic. It's not based on any sort of argument; I simply remember it. However, my belief that the European Union should not pursue a federal model – something like the United States of Europe – is based on a wide variety of arguments having to do with national identity, language, political structure, and cultural diversity.

Not all basic beliefs are *properly* basic. A belief is properly basic only if it can still be rational without arguments. My belief that there is a photograph of my wife on my desk does not need anything by way of argument: it is perfectly rational for me to believe it simply because I *see* it. It is, therefore, properly basic. Not so with my conviction that President Bolsonaro's political policy is currently hurting Brazil and the world. A mere feeling or hunch that this is so will not do to render that belief rational. It is rational only if it is based on data about the effects of his policy on nature, social cohesion, cultural heritage, political measures to deal with COVID-19, and so on.

Unsurprisingly, it is a matter of debate exactly when a belief is *properly* basic. In other words, it is a matter of debate when you need arguments for your belief and when you don't. It seems that

---

[5] I first explored this issue in a blog: "Can Atheism Be Properly Basic?," *Prosblogion: The Philosophy of Religion Blog*, March 21, 2015, https://web.archive.org/web/20170425123301/ http://prosblogion.ektopos.com/2015/03/21/can-atheism-be-properly-basic/.

many perceptual beliefs are properly basic: if you think you see a car, it is perfectly rational for you to believe you see one. You don't need any arguments for that. The same applies to many beliefs based on memory: if you believe you cycled to work this morning rather than going by train, that is a perfectly rational thing to believe even if you cannot produce any arguments for it. In fact, the list of beliefs that are properly basic seems virtually endless: that I was in Bologna this summer, that I am now working on a book manuscript, that I am more than 30 years old, that I feel well rested, that I exist, that the sun is shining today, that I enjoy sailing and trout fishing, and that I live in the Netherlands. These beliefs are perfectly rational even though they are not based on arguments. Of course, I could try to provide an argument for them, but whether or not I succeed in doing so is immaterial to their rationality.

Other beliefs are clearly not properly basic. If I believe, not on the basis of an argument but just because I feel that way, that COVID-19 vaccination is harmful to children or that there's human-induced climate change or that the Americans never landed on the moon, it seems that these beliefs are not properly basic. True, they are not based on arguments, but they *should* be in order to be rational. Some beliefs can be properly basic; others can't.

One more distinction from epistemology. There can be so-called *defeaters* for basic beliefs. Defeaters undermine the rationality of a belief. There are two main kinds of defeaters. *Rebutting* defeaters show that a belief is false. Thus, if you think you left your keys in your jacket, but you do not find them in your jacket upon going through your pockets, you thereby have a rebutting defeater. It is also possible to have an *undercutting* defeater. Crucially, it does not show that your belief is false, but it does give you reason to question your belief in the absence of further independent evidence.[6] Imagine you enter a factory and see a red widget on the assembly

---

[6] For more on defeaters, see, for instance, John Pollock, "Reliability and Justified Belief," *Canadian Journal of Philosophy* 14, no. 1 (1984): 103–114.

line. You therefore come to believe that there is a red widget on the assembly line. However, the factory owner then tells you that the widgets are being irradiated by various red lights, so that cracks invisible to the naked eye are detected. Consequently, all objects on the assembly line look red, even though only some of them are red – the others are yellow, pink, or blue. Looking at the widget in question, you have an undercutting defeater for your belief that it is red. After all, you now know that if you form this belief by looking at the widget's color, your belief is not reliably formed.

Here ends our little detour in epistemology. The crucial point is this: some beliefs require arguments in order to be rational whereas others don't. And even if a belief is properly basic and, therefore, doesn't require any arguments, we should accept it only if we don't encounter any serious defeaters for it.

Belief in God without Arguments

Let's return to Reformed epistemology for a moment. The movement claims that one can rationally believe that God exists even if one has no arguments whatsoever for God's existence. The idea behind this is as follows. *If* God exists, then there is a perfectly good and omnipotent being who created the world, including us. And if that's true, then it is not at all unlikely that God wants us to *know* that he exists. It seems implausible that only those who are able to construe complex arguments for God's existence would know that God exists. There would seem to be a bit of a tension with God's perfect goodness if he cared only about analytic philosophers and others with an IQ higher than 130 and a love for rigorous reasoning. Instead, it seems likely that God would have created human beings in such a way that they can more or less directly know that God exists – for instance, in prayer, in reading the Bible or other holy scriptures, in seeing the beauty of God's creation, in having a mystical experience, or maybe even without the belief having any sort of ground or basis, when it just spontaneously comes into existence.

In the wake of John Calvin, Alvin Plantinga calls the mechanism that would be responsible for the generation of such belief in God a *sensus divinitatis* (religious sense).[7] Reformed epistemologists, thus, tend to compare belief in God to beliefs based on memory, introspection, and perception: all these beliefs are normally perfectly rational even though they are not based on arguments – they are properly basic.

Needless to say, Reformed epistemology hasn't convinced everyone, not even all religious philosophers. Some Christian philosophers believe that in order for belief in God to be rational, the believer should be able to provide arguments for the existence of God. Yet, I think appearances may be a little deceiving here. More philosophers accept the basic tenets of Reformed epistemology than might initially seem. This is because many philosophers and theologians nowadays believe that there are rather strong arguments *against* the existence of God and that *because of that*, one needs arguments *for* God's existence. In other words, they think there are *defeaters* for belief in God. The things I have in mind here are the problem of evil, the problem of divine hiddenness, our contemporary knowledge of religious diversity, and secular psychological explanations of religious belief in terms of, say, wishful thinking or hyperactive agency detection. We will have a more careful look at many of them later on.

British philosopher Richard Swinburne has argued that belief in God can be rational only if arguments show that it is more likely than not to be true. Because the problem of evil provides such a challenge to belief in God, positive arguments for God's existence are needed. In a series of succinct and yet challenging volumes, he

---

[7] Since a similar idea can be found in the writings of such philosophers and theologians as Thomas Aquinas and John Calvin, Plantinga dubs this approach the Aquinas/ Calvin (A/C) model.

has defended such arguments in detail; for instance, the cosmo-logical argument, the fine-tuning argument, the argument from religious experience, the moral argument, and the argument from consciousness.[8] It seems, then, that most religious philosophers and atheists will agree that belief in God could be properly basic to begin with. But some of them, like Swinburne, believe in addition to that that some atheistic arguments are so strong that in their presence, belief in God can only be rational if there are also strong arguments in favor of God's existence. The real issue for them is whether there are any defeaters for belief in God that render it irrational.

Atheism without Arguments

Now it's time to turn to the real bone of contention: Can atheism also be properly basic? In other words, can one rationally believe that God does not exist even if one has no arguments against God's existence? Could there perhaps be atheistic experiences or intui-tions that render atheism rational?

In order to see whether this works, let us consider two sce-narios: one in which God exists and one in which God does not exist. Believers and atheists alike will agree that those are the two options – either God exists or he does not.

We can be rather brief about the scenario in which God *does* exist. If God exists and he is perfectly good, then he has probably created human beings in such a way that they can form the belief that God exists. It seems highly unlikely that he would have cre-ated human beings with a religious sense that normally leads to the belief that God does not exist, for he would then intentionally mislead all human beings. More importantly, even if that somehow could be the case, the mechanism producing atheistic belief would

---

[8] See especially Richard Swinburne, *The Existence of God*, 2nd ed. (Oxford: Clarendon, 2004).

be mistaken all the time – after all, God would exist. In fact, since God, according to mainstream Christianity, Islam, and Judaism, exists necessarily, the mechanism would necessarily be mistaken. It would inevitably produce false beliefs. Surely then, if God exists, one cannot know, let alone without any sort of argument, that God does not exist.

Naturally, I wouldn't expect the atheist to bet on this scenario anyway. I'd expect the atheist to rely on the scenario in which God does *not* exist. After all, that's what the atheist believes the world to be like: a world without gods.

In order to see whether this second option would work, consider an atheist's story about other properly basic beliefs – beliefs produced by seeing things, hearing sounds, remembering events, smelling odors, and introspecting oneself (noticing, for instance, that one longs for a pint of beer). Beliefs of this kind are perfectly rational even if one has no arguments for them.

But *why* are these beliefs properly basic? What stories can we tell to explain this? When it comes to the senses, memory, and introspection, one could say that these beliefs are properly basic because they are the result of the right causal interaction with our physical environment either outside us or within us. Beliefs based on seeing things, for instance, are usually true because visually perceiving our environment normally directly produces true beliefs. The most plausible explanation of why such perceptual beliefs are usually true will probably be one in terms of our evolutionary history. It seems evolutionarily advantageous to form true perceptual beliefs about our physical environment. If we didn't, we wouldn't have survived, and we wouldn't have reproduced. As American logician W. V. O. Quine eloquently put it, "Creatures inveterately wrong in their inductions have a pathetic but praiseworthy tendency to die before reproducing their kind."[9] If we failed to see a great white in the

---

[9] W. V. O. Quine, "Natural Kinds," in *Ontological Relativity and Other Essays* (New York: Columbia University Press, 1969), 126.

water beneath us or to notice a yawning abyss, our chances of survival would be somewhat on the low side. The same holds for other basic beliefs, such as those formed from memory or introspection: we'd be in trouble if we forgot where we have hidden the apples we collected or if we failed to notice that we're feeling dizzy. It also applies to basic mathematical beliefs, such as the belief that 2 + 2 = 4. Even if numbers are abstract entities that exist independently of us, we are still surrounded by no wolves, one wolf, two wolves, three wolves, or even more. Our physical interaction with our environment directly and automatically leads us to have certain basic mathematical beliefs, and it seems that having true basic mathematical beliefs will increase our chances of survival in many scenarios.[10]

Thus, on atheism, the story about why many of our beliefs are properly basic would be something like this: they have the right causal connection with the world outside or inside us, and having true beliefs contributes to survival. A few religious philosophers have questioned whether evolution indeed selects for true beliefs, but virtually all atheists wholeheartedly embrace this idea.[11] It seems to be the only game in town.

Now, the problem is that atheism seems rather different from our perceptual beliefs, auditory beliefs, introspective beliefs, and other basic beliefs. If the belief that God doesn't exist is to be a basic belief like perceptual or auditory beliefs, it would thus have to have the right causal connection with the world. But if God doesn't exist, he cannot cause anything in our physical environment, so there would be no causal connection between him and us. Nor would his

---

[10] For more-detailed accounts of why mathematical belief faculties are truth oriented and reliable, see the essays in Michael Potter, Mary Leng, and Alexander Paseau, eds., *Mathematical Knowledge* (Oxford: Oxford University Press, 2007). Others have argued that naturalism cannot even account for mathematical knowledge. See, for instance, Justin Clarke-Doane, *Morality and Mathematics* (Oxford: Oxford University Press, 2020). I'll leave that issue aside here.

[11] See especially the discussion on Alvin Plantinga's evolutionary argument against atheism in James Beilby, ed., *Naturalism Defeated? Essays on Plantinga's Evolutionary Argument against Naturalism* (Ithaca: Cornell University Press, 2002).

nonexistence be materialized in the way a property like *there being three wolves within a range of twenty feet* can be. How, then, could we ever know that there is no God?

Of course, believing that God does not exist may have survival value. Just to be clear: scientists tend to think the opposite.[12] They think belief in God rather than atheism has survival value. Belief in God has survival value, for instance, because it creates social cohesion among groups, or because it makes people behave better if they feel they are watched all the time. But even if somehow atheism has survival value as well, it is hard to see how it could have such value in virtue of things that have to do with truth. Atheism may make you, say, courageous or independent. But it would not stand in the causal connection required for tracking the truth about the nonexistence of God.

It starts to look, then, as if there's a remarkable *asymmetry* between belief in God on the one hand and atheism on the other. Belief in God can be perfectly rational even without any arguments. All the religious believer needs to do is deflate the arguments against belief in God. Not so with atheism: atheism can be rational only if the atheist has some serious arguments against God's existence.[13] I've got to say that I find this rather

---

[12] We already saw that Jesse Bering suggests that belief in God is produced by an evolutionarily advantageous Hyperactive Agency Detection Device. David Sloan Wilson argues that religious belief, including theistic belief, is evolutionarily advantageous for groups of people; see David Sloan Wilson, *Darwin's Cathedral: Evolution, Religion, and the Nature of Society* (Chicago: University of Chicago Press, 2002).

[13] For those readers who have a background in analytic philosophy or simply a penchant for rigorous argumentation, here's the argument in a somewhat more formal version:

  (1) One's basic belief that *p* is prima facie rational if and only if it's epistemically possible that one's belief that *p* is produced by a reliable truth-oriented cognitive mechanism. [prem.]

  (2) It's epistemically possible that God exists and that he has created humans with a reliable truth-oriented cognitive mechanism producing the basic belief that God exists. [prem.]

surprising myself. Some may even think that it's unfair. Maybe it is. But if our reflections here are right, that's just how it is. Atheism is simply very different from theism, and this is an inevitable consequence. That it has this consequence is because it's a negative belief with an extremely ambitious scope. The atheist will have to accept the asymmetry between theism and atheism. In fact, if all this is right, maybe there is no presumption of atheism but a presumption of theism.

But perhaps things are not that simple. There's much that the atheist can say in reply. Let's delve into that and see whether there's a way to escape the argument. In doing so, we'll run into some tough philosophical reasoning, more so than in the other chapters.

(3) One's belief that God exists is prima facie rational, even if one has no arguments for God's existence. [from (1), (2)]

(4) Either God exists or he doesn't. [prem.]

(5) It is epistemically impossible that, if God exists, one's basic belief that God doesn't exist is produced by a *reliable* truth-oriented cognitive mechanism. [prem.]

(6) It's epistemically impossible that, if God does *not* exist, one's basic belief that God doesn't exist is produced by a reliable *truth-oriented* cognitive mechanism. [prem.]

(7) It's epistemically impossible that one's basic belief that God doesn't exist is produced by a reliable truth-oriented cognitive mechanism. [from (4), (5), (6)]

(8) One's belief that God doesn't exist is either basic or nonbasic. [prem.]

(9) One's basic belief that God doesn't exist can be prima facie rational only if one has arguments against the existence of God. [from (1), (7), (8)]

(10) If one's belief that p can be prima facie rational even if one doesn't have any arguments for p, whereas one's belief that q can be prima facie rational only if one has arguments for q, then p and q are epistemically asymmetrical. [def.]

(11) Theism and atheism are epistemically asymmetrical. [from (3), (9), (10)]

I speak about epistemic rather than metaphysical possibility because it seems plausible that if God exists, he exists necessarily, and if he doesn't exist, he necessarily doesn't exist. By *epistemic possibility* I mean that something is possible *for all we know*. I've defended premises (1) and (2) above. Premise (3) follows from (1) and (2). The law of the excluded middle implies premise (4). I have defended (5) and (6) above. Premise (7) follows logically from (4), (5), and (6). Premise (8) is also implied by the law of the excluded middle. Premise (9) follows from (1), (7), and (8). Premise (10) captures a plausible definition of epistemic asymmetry, and (11) follows from (3), (9), and (10).

I promise, though, that through this challenging exercise, we'll truly get a better grip on how atheism works and what makes atheism and religious belief stand out from a range of other beliefs, from a belief in an empty chair to belief in bigfoot.

Experiencing the Absence of God

Atheists may suggest there are certain experiences that make atheism rational even in the absence of arguments for atheism. What I have in mind are phenomena that seem to count against God's existence, things like experiencing the evil and the harshness of life or the utter indifference of the cosmos toward human beings.[14]

Now, an experience is, at least phenomenologically, an experience *of something*. We don't experience a thing that doesn't exist – even though we might mistakenly think so. Therefore, if there are atheistic experiences, they are experiences of something, such as harshness, suffering, or indifference. Even an experience of what might seem to be nothing is always an experience of something – for example, an empty room or an empty space. This means that there is a gap to be filled. How do we get from the atheistic experience of, say, suffering or indifference on the one hand to atheism on the other? The atheist needs some kind of argument to get from those experiences to atheism. Such arguments will involve steps like the idea that a perfectly good God would never allow such suffering or that an omnipotent God would somehow prevent such suffering. Of course, such arguments may be entirely legitimate. But the point here is that if arguments are needed to get from atheistic experiences to atheism, then, by definition, the belief that God does not exist will not be basic. So, it seems that experience all by itself can never justify atheism.

---

[14] The idea that experiencing evil might noninferentially lead to the belief that God does not exist is also mentioned by Plantinga, *Warranted Christian Belief*, 484, and defended by Paul Draper, "Evil and the Proper Basicality of Belief in God," *Faith and Philosophy* 8, no. 2 (1991): 141.

What about the experience that matter is all there is? Judaism, Islam, and Christianity say that God is a spiritual being. So, if only the material cosmos exists, it does indeed follow that there is no God. It's hard to see, however, what an experience that matter is all there is would amount to. One can experience this bit of matter – say, all the matter in the room in which I'm writing this book – or that bit of matter or a whole series of material entities – for example, one can look at a desert landscape or even at the earth from a distance. But that is still different from experiencing that matter is all there is. It seems that one can only think, believe, or have the intuition that matter is all there is, rather than experience this. But if it's a belief or intuition rather than an experience, we face the same old problem: it's unclear how, on an entirely atheistic story, such a belief could be rational if it is not based on any kind of argument.

Don't get me wrong – I don't want to disqualify experiences of suffering, emptiness, evil, or the harshness of life. In fact, I think we should take them much more seriously in public debates. Here, I'm merely making a philosophical point about them: they can never by themselves justify atheism. One also needs arguments for atheism in order to render atheism rational.

But maybe we're going too fast here. Although we apparently cannot experience the nonexistence of God, can we not *fail to* experience God? Can atheistic belief not be rational if it results simply from *not experiencing* God? Many atheists will readily claim that they've never experienced God. They may grant that they have had religious experiences, but then add that they've found purely naturalistic explanations for them. They never truly experienced God. Cannot that all by itself justify atheism?

I'm afraid the answer has to be negative. To be sure, it's possible that atheists never experience anything of God.[15] However, it is a

---

[15] Or, put slightly more carefully, that is *epistemically* possible. If we talk about *metaphysical* possibility, we should distinguish between object perception and fact perception. If God exists, then it may well be metaphysically impossible that

rather large step from not experiencing God to the belief that God does not exist. It may be that God has not yet revealed himself to the atheist. Or maybe God reveals himself only to some people, for whatever reason. Now, one might think that a perfectly good God would have to reveal himself to everyone, atheists included – the sooner the better. That, however, is a questionable and in fact highly debated assumption, as the literature on the argument from divine hiddenness shows. The basic idea in this argument is that a perfectly good God wouldn't hide himself, but clearly, he *does*, at least from some people at some times. As the literature shows, though, that premise is far from evident.[16] I'm not saying that it's false; it may well be true. What I want to say is simply this: if some kind of argument is needed to get from not experiencing God to the belief that God does not exist, then one's atheism is no longer basic. In other words, it may still be rational, but only if it is based on arguments for atheism. We still haven't been able to establish a presumption of atheism.

But isn't there also an argumentative gap between *theistic* experiences and the existence of God? Isn't Christianity, for instance, in the same boat as atheism? After all, what many people describe as experiences of God are really experiences of the splendor of the Grand Teton, the regularity and order in the cosmos, or the beauty of Bach's "Erbarme dich, mein Gott," of feeling addressed by a passage in the Gospels or being overwhelmed by a miraculous healing

the atheist never has an object perception of God, because it may conflict with God's perfect goodness if he doesn't reveal himself in one way or another to each human being. However, even if God exists, it may be that atheists never have a fact perception of God, that is, never take any of their experiences to be an experience of God. For the distinction between fact perception (or epistemic perception, as Dretske calls it) and object perception (or nonepistemic perception), see Fred I. Dretske, *Seeing and Knowing* (London: Routledge & Kegan Paul, 1969).

[16] For several arguments against this assumption, see, for instance, Daniel Howard-Snyder and Paul K. Moser, eds., *Divine Hiddenness: New Essays* (Cambridge: Cambridge University Press, 2002). See also Herman Philipse, *God in the Age of Science? A Critique of Religious Reason* (Oxford: Oxford University Press, 2012), 302–309.

or the birth of a child. The content of such an experience is that the snowy mountain is beautiful or that the stars move steadily along the sky. Thus, all by themselves, these experiences don't imply the existence of God. It seems one would need some further premises in order to get to the conclusion that God exists.[17] If that's true, then religious belief faces the same challenge as atheism: it's rational only if based on serious arguments.

Upon further consideration, however, it turns out that religious experiences are actually quite different from atheistic experiences. Many religious believers, certain philosophers included, claim that there are mystical experiences in which people experience God directly. They experience him mystically or feel his presence by way of a sixth, religious sense.[18] The idea is that humans are endowed with a unique mechanism for experiencing God (perhaps we could indeed call this a sensus divinitatis), a mechanism different from vision, smell, hearing, touch, taste, and introspection. Surely, this is not unlikely if God does indeed exist.

Can one really perceive God, though? According to monotheistic religions, God is infinite – in goodness, in power, in glory, maybe even in beauty. By contrast, whatever we are, we are clearly not infinite, and our perception is rather limited. How, then, could religious experience by itself make belief in God rational?

It seems to me that most religious believers would affirm that they cannot perceive God in his infinity. Yet, a simple philosophical distinction can be helpful here. This is the distinction between *de re* and *de facto*, a distinction often made in metaphysics, epistemology, and philosophy of language. We may not be able to perceive *that* God is infinite (*de facto*). Yet, we *may* very well be able to perceive part of *a God who is in fact infinite* (*de re*). Maybe if we

---

[17] For this line of reasoning, see Nicholas Everitt, *The Non-existence of God* (London: Routledge, 2004), 26–28.

[18] For a description of some of these experiences, see Kai-Man Kwan, "The Argument from Religious Experience," in *The Blackwell Companion to Natural Theology*, ed. William Lane Craig and J. P. Moreland (Oxford: Wiley-Blackwell, 2012), 499–501.

perceive an infinite God, the belief simply arises that there is an infinite God. That could be the workings of a sensus divinitatis. For all I can see, then, religious experiences may well make belief in God rational, even in the absence of arguments. Unless, of course, there are defeaters.

In fact, it may not even be necessary to perceive God himself. Imagine that Alvin forms the basic belief that God exists upon experiencing the beauty of the Grand Teton. If God exists, then it isn't at all unlikely that he has created in Alvin a mechanism that brings about belief in God when Al sees the beauty of the Grand Teton. Why would such a mechanism only produce belief in God when one perceives God himself and not when one perceives "the works of his hands," or the vestiges of God (*vestigia Dei*), as Augustine calls them? The religious sense would be entirely accurate in such a case. Thus, even if people can't experience God directly, belief in God can still be properly basic – it can be rational without arguments.

Probably, not all atheists will be convinced by this. A common move is to point out that monotheists are atheists with regard to all other gods except their own, for they believe that all the other gods, such as the many gods of ancient Greece or those of Hinduism, don't exist. Says Dawkins:

> I have found it an amusing strategy, when asked whether I am an atheist, to point out that the questioner is also an atheist when considering Zeus, Apollo, Amon Ra, Mithras, Baal, Thor, Wotan, the Golden Calf and the Flying Spaghetti Monster. I just go one god further.[19]

The religious believer, then, needs a pretty much infinite number of arguments to show that all these other gods don't exist. Thus, the atheist is worse off only with regard to a single god. With respect to all the other gods, the atheist and the theist are on a par.[20]

---

[19] Richard Dawkins, *The God Delusion* (London: Bantam, 2006), 53.
[20] I thank Herman Philipse for leveling this objection. For a written version of this point, see Philipse, *God in the Age of Science?*, vii.

A slightly more sophisticated version of this objection may even appeal to etymological considerations: Christians were originally called *atheos* – "godless" – because they rejected the Roman gods of the time. This nicely fits the ideal of courage and intellectual heroism that we explored earlier: since you are an atheist with regard to all the other gods, you need just that little bit of courage to take the final step and reject also your own god, which is what a consistent and adventurous person would do. What Dutch atheist Herman Philipse says is another good illustration of this argument:

> Apologetic philosophers of religion must also be critical ones, since each religious doctrine being to some extent logically incompatible with many others, in arguing for the truth of one creed they must argue against its religious rivals. Indeed, most religious believers are atheists with regard to deities of other religions, since they deny the existence of these deities, although typically polytheists will be more inclusive and tolerant than monotheists as regards this point. People who are usually called "atheists" are in fact universal atheists, in contrast with the particular and selective atheism of religious believers.[21]

And British philosopher A. C. Grayling cashes it out in terms of "one more god to go":

> Everybody is an atheist about almost all gods, the difference between true atheists and Christians or Muslims being that the latter still have one more god to go, one more god to stop believing in.[22]

The argument is often repeated in the literature.[23] Yet, I've seen better ones. Christians are not atheists with regard to other religions – that's simply not what it means to be an atheist. The Oxford English

[21] Philipse, *God in the Age of Science?*, xii.

[22] A. C. Grayling, *The God Argument: The Case against Religion and for Humanism* (London: Bloomsbury, 2013), 33.

[23] See, for instance, Michael Shermer, "How to Think about God: Theism, Atheism, and Science," in *50 Voices of Disbelief: Why We Are Atheists*, ed. Russell Blackford and Udo Schüklenk (Oxford: Wiley-Blackwell, 2009), 72.

Dictionary defines *atheist* as "one who denies or disbelieves the existence of a God." Since, say, Muslims *do* believe in the existence of a God, they simply aren't atheists. A man who is married to only one wife is *not* a bachelor, not even a bachelor with respect to all other women. That's just not what it means to be a bachelor. Similarly, a Muslim is not an atheist, not even an atheist with respect to all the other gods that she doesn't believe in. To claim that she is, is simply to be semantically confused – whether intentionally or unintentionally so. Also, if the monotheistic god of Islam exists, then clearly Zeus does not exist. So, one doesn't need an argument against the existence of all the other gods in order to rationally believe in God.

What underlies this objection is a particular view of what it is to have religious faith. To have faith, so the idea seems to be, is to embrace a particular set of statements about God as true and to reject all other statements about him as (utterly) false. This may well be true of some varieties of religions, certain kinds of fundamentalism in particular. But it's not at all representative of religious faith in general. Many religions are *henotheistic*: they worship one particular god or several particular gods while not denying the existence of others. Early Judaism was also henotheistic: it worshipped Yahweh while acknowledging the existence of other gods, like Baal and Astarte – with various qualifications, such as that they are deaf and mute. Monotheistic religions nowadays are primarily *monolatristic*: they demand the worship of only one god. While not accepting the existence of the many gods of polytheistic religions, they acknowledge that God also reveals himself and is present in other religions. One should not confuse monotheism with a dogmatic rejection of all religious ideas from all other religions.

Most Christians are drawn toward God as he is portrayed in the Christian tradition. But when Muslims worship God as the perfectly good creator of the universe, Christians generally don't think that Muslims are misguided in doing so. Of course, many of them think that Muslims have a deficient or incomplete image of God. They take it, for instance, that God has revealed himself decisively in Jesus Christ and that this makes a pivotal difference to how we think of God. However, they surely don't reject the idea, crucial to Islam, that there is a God, that he is the creator of the universe, and that he is perfect in all regards. Thus, they reject not so much all the gods of other religions as *particular conceptions of God* found in other religions. They discard them as false, deficient, or incomplete – to the extent that they hold views about that at all.[24] Naturally, many Christians and other monotheists tend to think that the millions of gods worshipped in Hinduism don't really exist. But that leaves plenty of room for truth, insight, and legitimate worship of the transcendent, the creator, a good God, and so on, in other religions. In fact, there is a whole subdiscipline in Christian theology called *missiology* that explores how the Christian faith relates to other religions and how God reveals himself in other faiths.

There seems to be an important difference, then, between religious experience and atheistic experience. Is there a way atheistic experiences could make atheism rational?

Belief That Something Doesn't Exist

The atheist still has some cards up his sleeve. Don't we have all sorts of beliefs about the nonexistence of objects without any arguments? When I see an empty chair, I immediately form the basic belief that there is no one sitting on the chair. In other words, there is no human being on the chair. That's a belief about nonexistence: the nonexistence of a human on that chair at that time. I really don't need any kind of argument for that. I simply *see* that there isn't anyone on the chair. And when I'm in my living room, I see at once that there is no elephant in the room (if you can't, your living room

---

[24] Jeroen de Ridder and René van Woudenberg defend this in much more detail in "Referring to, Believing in, and Worshipping the Same God: A Reformed View," *Faith and Philosophy* 31, no. 1 (2014): 46–67.

is probably a little bigger than mine). I need no argument for that belief – it is basic and perfectly rational.

The problem with these examples is that they all concern beliefs about the nonexistence of some object at some place. We can reliably form beliefs about whether there's someone on the chair or whether there is an elephant in the room without any sort of argument because we can *oversee* the chair and the room. With the existence of God, however, things are different. God is supposed to be immaterial; that is, he is without a physical body. By using your eyes, then, you're not going to see God. Also, we don't have the kind of overview over the entirety of reality that we have over the chair, the room, and even larger physical objects, such as the earth or distant galaxies.[25] We can't oversee reality at once. Not seeing God is crucially different from not seeing someone in the chair or not seeing an elephant in the room.[26]

But monotheists might not be off the hook that quickly. God, on the classical Christian or Muslim or Judaic conception of God, is supposed to be *omnipresent*, which means God is thought to be everywhere at any time. That's one of his alleged perfections. And if he's everywhere, he's also here. Thus, if he's not here, he's not everywhere. Hence, if God – on the classical conception – doesn't exist here, he exists nowhere.[27] Short line of reasoning, big result.

[25] Jerome I. Gellman, "A New Look at the Problem of Evil," *Faith and Philosophy 9*, no. 2 (1992): 210–216. In his *Experience of God and the Rationality of Theistic Belief* (Ithaca: Cornell University Press, 1997), 76–83, Gellman fails to take this point into account in his description of alleged cases of experiencing the nonexistence of God.

[26] Of course, we also hold beliefs about the nonexistence of things that don't concern a specific location in the way my belief that there is no one on the chair does. Here, we can think of such beliefs as that the yeti doesn't exist, that phlogiston doesn't exist, that quasi dragons don't exist, and that Venusians don't exist. Note, though, that those beliefs aren't basic: they are based on arguments – some kind of inference – to the effect that these entities do not exist. We argue, for instance, that if the yeti existed, there would be evidence for his existence in certain mountainous areas, but that there is no such evidence and that we, therefore, have good reason to think that the yeti does not exist.

[27] I thank Brian Leftow for raising this objection.

I find this an intriguing idea. Yet, I'm not convinced. Of course, we are talking here about a highly specific conception of God and a particular attribute. If there's no omnipresent God, that would hardly justify the claim that there are no gods whatsoever. And that there are no gods whatsoever is exactly what atheism claims. Thus, atheism could never be a basic belief. It's also not immediately clear what the attribute of omnipresence is supposed to amount to. If you have the time to delve into systematic theology, you'll soon discover many different accounts of omnipresence. Crucially, many of them suggest that *omnipresence* doesn't mean that God is physically present everywhere.[28] And only physical presence is the sort of thing we can perceive with our eyes. As I said, though, on classical monotheistic conceptions, God is not a material but a spiritual being. And if God is a spiritual being, it should not be surprising that we can't see him at specific locations. Therefore, if one fails to see God at a particular time and place, that can never all by itself make atheism rational.

Atheism on Testimony

Maybe we've approached atheism too individualistically so far. It would be absurd to think that atheism normally arises in splendid isolation. Many of our beliefs don't. I believe, for instance, that the Gobi Desert is in southern Mongolia and that Boyle's law holds, but I've never been to Mongolia and I've never tested Boyle's law. I believe these things on the basis of people's testimony in articles, books, dictionaries, and stories. The same is true for countless other beliefs that I have: they aren't based on arguments but on people's testimony. And yet, they are perfectly rational. Couldn't atheism be like that?

To be sure, there's a lot of testimony about the nonexistence of God. Louise Antony's *Philosophers without Gods*, for instance,

---

[28] See, for instance, Luco J. van den Brom, *Divine Presence in the World: A Critical Analysis of the Notion of Divine Omnipresence* (Kampen: Kok, 1993).

contains 20 testimonies to the effect that there is no God, and Russell Blackford and Udo Schüklenk's *50 Voices of Disbelief* contains, well, 50 of them.[29] Could one's belief that God doesn't exist be rational on a testimonial basis of this kind? After all, it is often wise to base one's belief on solid testimony. In fact, many religious people do exactly the same: they ground their beliefs in the testimony of their pastor, their parents, or a friend, or in that of the apostle Luke in the New Testament.

When someone who has been there herself tells me that the Gobi Desert is in southern Mongolia, I've got plenty of reason to trust her. After all, some people travel over long distances, and – I presume – I've got no reason to think she's lying. Similarly, when a scientist tells me that Boyle's law is correct, I've got no reason to mistrust her, for scientists are the kind of people who know such things. But now imagine that an atheist tells me that God doesn't exist. Why should I believe him? He could be an expert physicist, a world-class politician, even a Nobel Prize winner, but how's that relevant? The atheist might be an expert in the philosophy of religion, but there are at least as many experts in that field who are religious. So, why should I accept his atheistic testimony?

The atheist might not give any arguments against God's existence but just repeat that he believes there's no God. Well, merely believing someone because he claims something isn't a proper way to form one's beliefs. If one accepts the testimony of the atheist in this situation, surely one's belief is not rational.

Alternatively, the atheist could give various arguments against God's existence. Maybe there are such good arguments for atheism; we'll turn to them later in this book. If you buy into these arguments and come to accept atheism on that basis, your belief is, clearly, based on arguments. In other words, your atheism will no longer be basic.

[29] See Louise M. Antony, ed., *Philosophers without Gods: Meditations on Atheism and the Secular Life* (Oxford: Oxford University Press, 2007); Russell Blackford and Udo Schüklenk, eds., *50 Voices of Disbelief: Why We Are Atheists* (Oxford: Wiley-Blackwell, 2009).

This leaves only one option: the atheist could give arguments that are too complicated for you to understand. I don't think this is all that strange – I often rely on complicated arguments of others, such as scientists, policy makers, and journalists. The problem with this particular situation, though, is that any well-educated person living in a Western society knows that there are many others who do believe in God and who are not convinced by those atheistic arguments. When I trust a scientist with respect to global warming, I can rationally do so because the vast majority of experts – some 97 percent – believe in human-induced climate change. With atheism, things are different: experts, such as theologians and philosophers of religion, deeply disagree with one another. And that is well-known. Atheistic testimony just doesn't work the way that scientific testimony does.

What about religious belief and testimony, then? Well, a divinely implanted religious sense could well be designed to produce belief in God upon the right sort of testimony. So, we cannot rule out that belief in God can be rational if based on testimony, such as the testimony of the apostles or that of holy scriptures. Of course, such belief based on testimony should not be indiscriminate; it shouldn't accept any sort of utterly nonsensical testimony, for instance. Still, religious belief can be properly based on testimony rather than on arguments. That's a crucial difference with atheism based on testimony: atheism still needs arguments in order to be rational.

Belief in Exotic Beings

If belief in God can be rational in the absence of any serious arguments, doesn't that mean that anything goes? Someone could believe that Alpha Centurions visited our planet in the distant past and implanted in human beings a mechanism that produces the belief that Alpha Centurions exist. This could've happened, and there's no reason to think that Alpha Centurions don't exist on some distant planet. So, the belief that there are Alpha Centurions would be rational. But clearly, it isn't. So, even if we're not able to show where the argument goes wrong, this *reductio ad absurdum* makes clear it is somehow deficient.

There's a natural explanation, though, for why such a belief is irrational: there are *defeaters* for the belief that there are Alpha Centurions. The person having this belief would, for instance, have a hard time explaining why *she* believes in Alpha Centurions while virtually nobody else does. It would be difficult to clarify why the Alpha Centurions left no other traces of their visit and why, apart from her belief, we have no evidence for their existence. Of course, something similar might apply to belief in God. Maybe there are good defeaters for belief in God. We can't simply assume either that there are or that there aren't.[30]

Now that we're in the business of exploring exotic beings anyway, how should we think of the many earthly creatures that people believe in and that atheists like to draw our attention to? What I have in mind are such things as fairies, unicorns, trolls, the yeti, and bigfoot. Any reasonable person would want to say that belief in them is irrational. Can the asymmetry between belief in God and atheism that we've explored so far do justice to that?

I think it can. On the one hand, the existence of these strange creatures has a much lower prior probability than the existence of God. Judaism, Christianity, and Islam understand God as a perfect, necessarily existent being who created the universe and everything it contains. These other beings are just contingent, often with an exotic or even absurd set of properties. They are, therefore, a priori much

---

[30] Alternatively, one might say that belief in Alpha Centurions is not all-things-considered rational because there is no favoring evidence for their existence, whereas there *is* favoring evidence in such cases as believing that there is a grapefruit in front of you. For the notion of favoring evidence, see Duncan Pritchard, "Relevant Alternatives, Perceptual Knowledge, and Discrimination," *Noûs* 44, no. 2 (2010): 245–268. This line of thought regarding such beliefs as belief in Alpha Centurions and belief in the Great Pumpkin is developed and defended by Kyle Scott, "Return of the Great Pumpkin," *Religious Studies* 50, no. 3 (2014): 297–308.

less likely to exist. The evidence for their existence would have to be really impressive for belief in them to be rational. On the other hand, there is simply too much evidence that defeats belief in these creatures. For one thing, if the sightings of bigfoot in Oregon were genuine, there would have to be a fairly large population of big-foots – otherwise, they'd die out pretty quickly. Also, there would be evidence of their existence: many more sightings, recordings, traces they leave from hunting, sleeping, and eating. That there aren't any such things gives us more than enough reason to think that bigfoot doesn't exist. Belief in such a creature is, therefore, irrational.

A Presumption of What?

It's time to wrap up. We've explored whether there's a presumption of atheism. In other words, we've looked at whether we should presume atheism to be true unless there are really strong arguments for the existence of gods. This presumption is championed by such atheists as Antony Flew, Sam Harris, Aaron Holland, Michael Martin, Michael Scriven, and Michael Tooley.[31]

It turned out that there's a remarkable asymmetry between belief that God exists and belief that there is no God. While belief in God can be rational even if there are no arguments for God's existence, atheism can be rational only if the atheist has arguments against the existence of God. This is crucial. For it means that all that the theist needs to do is rebut the arguments against God's existence and against belief in God. The atheist, by contrast, not only needs to refute the arguments for the existence of God and against believing that there is no God but also needs to provide arguments against the existence of God. I find this a surprising result of our exploration. As I said, it might seem unfair. But I'm afraid that's just the way it is. A careful look into the epistemology of theism and atheism reveals

---

[31] Three Michaels. *Michael* means "Who is like God?" What's in a name?

that things have to be this way – it just follows from what theism and atheism say.

John Mackie claims there's no clear onus of proof in the debate between theists and atheists: both have a duty to provide arguments in favor of their position. I believe that such arguments exist and that they have great value. But if I'm right, there's an important sense in which Mackie is mistaken. The theist can, but *need not* provide arguments for what she believes. The atheist, however, will be rational only if what he says can be backed up by argument. Don't get me wrong – I'd really love to hear more in public debates about the various experiences that have led atheists to the belief that there's no God. As I said, I think we should talk more about them, which is why we've spent so much time in this book getting to better understand such experiences. Yet, whatever they are, they cannot make atheism rational. It all boils down to the arguments atheists can give against belief in God.

But shouldn't we in general presume that something doesn't exist unless we have good evidence for its existence? This is what John Harris suggests:

> Where there are no good reasons to believe something is the case, the rational conclusion to come to is that it is not the case, not that it may or may not be the case. There are so many fantastical things that I *could* believe but which I do not entertain for a moment because there simply is no reason, or no remotely adequate reason, to suppose them true or even probable. That is surely the case with God.[32]

Let's leave the "no remotely adequate reason" clause aside here and zoom in on the underlying issue. Is it true that if you have no reason to believe in something, you should believe that it doesn't exist?

---

[32] John Harris, "Wicked or Dead? Reflections on the Moral Character and Existential Status of God," in *50 Voices of Disbelief*, ed. Russell Blackford and Udo Schüklenk (Oxford: Wiley-Blackwell, 2009), 34.

I'm afraid the answer is no. We don't have good evidence to believe in the existence of extraterrestrial life. But surely that doesn't make it rational to believe that there's no extraterrestrial life. Until we come across some really good evidence, we should *suspend judgment* on whether there's extraterrestrial life. There's also no good evidence that the number of planets in the universe is odd. Assuming that the number of planets is finite rather than infinite and definite rather than vague, their number is either even or odd. Does rationality require us to believe that their number is even? No, of course not. We should therefore *suspend judgment* on whether the number of planets is odd.

The atheist might retort that the existence of God is a priori improbable. By that, I mean that it's unlikely, independently of all the empirical evidence. One might think, for instance, that the very concept of God is incoherent and that that makes atheism rational unless we find good arguments for the existence of God.[33] An example is the well-known objection that if God is omnipotent, he can create a stone that he cannot lift. If he can create such a stone, he's not omnipotent; and if he cannot create such a stone, he's not omnipotent either. Maybe these a priori objections are sound. The problem, though, is that we obviously would need some sort of argument for the claim that the existence of God is a priori improbable or that the concept of God is incoherent. Thus, even though atheism could be rational in that case, it would still not be a basic belief. The atheist has to come up with arguments against God's existence. So, the point stands: theism can be rational without arguments, but atheism can be rational only if it is based on arguments.

I think we may want to go one step further than just rejecting the presumption of atheism. Of course, I didn't argue that rationality

---

[33] The latter, of course, requires that one solve most of the problems regarding the coherence of the concept of God. For it's hard to see how arguments for the existence of something would make it rational to believe in it if there's good reason to think that the very concept of that thing is incoherent.

requires all humans to assume that God exists until they find good arguments against his existence. I don't think that's a defensible claim. Many people lack the experiences and intuitions to believe this in the first place. However, those who've had such experiences or intuitions and feel themselves led to belief in God can perfectly rationally stick to that even if they don't have any arguments for God's existence. They'd only need to be able to deflate arguments against belief in God – arguments having to do with suffering, the hiddenness of God, the alleged tensions between science and religion, and much more. We'll come back to that in due course.

Given this crucial asymmetry, it is no exaggeration to say that we've stumbled upon something like the presumption of theism – not of atheism, but of theism. That is truly surprising. Imagine that belief in objective moral truths would need no arguments while moral constructivism would, or that political conservatism would need no arguments whereas political liberalism would. In fact, that would be so remarkable that it's hard to even imagine such a situation. But we've uncovered good reason to think this situation holds for belief in God in comparison with atheism.

If atheistic experiences can't really justify atheism, if the cognitive frameworks that naturally lead to atheism have serious deficiencies, and if we can't just presume that God does not exist, the tenability of atheism boils down to arguments against belief in God. It's time, then, to turn to those arguments and see whether they hold water and what we can learn from them.

5 | Atheistic Arguments and Faith

We Should Welcome Atheistic Arguments

Arguments for atheism have received plenty of attention.[1] Yet, as I was reconsidering them over the last few years, something struck me about these arguments: some of them are really not at all arguments against belief in God. Either they work with an image of God that in no way matches mainstream monotheism, or they employ an idea of religious belief that doesn't correspond at all with what it's really like for people to believe in God. Yet, they are of crucial value, because they dismantle misguided ideas about belief in God. In fact, I'm starting to think that there is something deeply religious about these arguments. They help humanity to overcome primitive ideas about God and about faith in God. They guide us in steering away from fundamentalism and making room for a more mature and profound faith in God. It's my impression that many religious believers tend to avoid serious reflection on atheistic arguments. If I'm right, they should instead welcome them, delve into them, and come out of that process with a purified and richer faith. Those who seriously consider religious faith may find them helpful to sort out what is tenable and what isn't. So, let's consider these arguments in more detail: what do they teach us? Some of them give us insights into the nature of religious faith. Others, we shall see, shed light on how to understand the nature and character of God.

---

[1] In fact, I've discussed many of them in detail elsewhere. See Stefan Paas and Rik Peels, *God bewijzen: Argumenten voor en tegen geloven* [Why it's OK to believe in God] (Amsterdam: Balans, 2013).

Kinds of Arguments for Atheism

There are two kinds of arguments for atheism: arguments against belief in God and arguments against God's existence. Arguments against belief in God aim to show that belief in God is problematic, for instance, because it is irrational, whether or not there is a God. Arguments against God's existence are meant to show that belief in God is false. Of course, in the end, they are meant to do the same thing, namely, to make sure people give up belief in God or don't embrace religious faith in the first place. But the ways in which they attempt to achieve this are crucially different, and it's good to keep that in mind. We shall first zoom in on arguments against belief in God.

There's another, equally important way to distinguish the various arguments for atheism, namely, by dividing them into *epistemic arguments* and *moral arguments*. Epistemic arguments have to do with truth and falsehood: they are intended to show that God doesn't exist, that belief in God is irrational or illusory, or some such thing. The aim of moral arguments is to show that belief in God is immoral, either because God, as portrayed in some religions, is an abject being, or because belief in God or faith in God is immoral. Their aim is not to show that there is no God or that faith is unreasonable but to show that it would be immoral to believe in that sort of god, that religious faith is harmful in various ways. Whether or not God exists, a decent human being should steer clear of belief in God. Here's an example of a moral argument, provided by Christopher Hitchens:

> When I say, as the subtitle of my book, that I think religion poisons everything, I'm not just doing what publishers like and coming up with a provocative subtitle, I mean to say it infects us in our most basic integrity. It says we can't be moral without Big Brother, without a totalitarian permission. It means we can't be good to one another, it means we can't think without this. We must be afraid, we must also be forced to love someone who we fear, the essence

of sado-masochism and the essence of abjection, the essence of the master-slave relationship and that knows that death is coming and can't wait to bring it on. I say this is evil. And though I do, some nights, stay at home, I enjoy more the nights when I go out and fight against this ultimate wickedness and ultimate stupidity.[2]

Clearly, epistemic and moral arguments are not unrelated. Believing in all sorts of falsehoods and embracing plain irrationality can have endless harmful consequences and thus be, in some sense, morally wrong. Yet, it is helpful to keep them apart. The British philosopher Alain de Botton, founder of the widely popular School of Life, for instance, thinks that religion is actually morally enhancing because of its rituals and practices that contribute to human flourishing. Yet, he calls himself an atheist because he takes it to be obvious that there is no God. At the outset of his book *Religion for Atheists*, he says:

> To save time, and at the risk of losing readers painfully early on in this project, let us bluntly state that of course no religions are true in any God-given sense…. The real issue is not whether God exist or not, but where to take the argument once one decides that he evidently doesn't. The premise of this book is that it must be possible to remain a committed atheist and nevertheless find religions sporadically useful, interesting and consoling – and be curious as to the possibilities of importing certain of their ideas and practices into the secular realm.[3]

Despite their shared atheism, the stark contrast in tone between Hitchens and de Botton should be clear. Hitchens believes religion is the root of all evil, whereas de Botton sees much of moral and

---

[2] See the transcript of the Hitchens vs. Turek debate at Virginia Commonwealth University, September 8, 2008, at http://hitchensdebates.blogspot.com/2010/11/hitchens-vs-turek-vcu.html.

[3] Alain de Botton, *Religion for Atheists: A Non-believer's Guide to the Uses of Religion* (London: Hamish Hamilton, 2012), 11–12.

spiritual value in religious ideas, rituals, and practices. De Botton's objection to faith in God is entirely epistemic (religion is clearly false), not moral.

There's one category of atheistic arguments that we won't delve into here. It's the category of philosophical a priori objections to belief in God. For instance, Moritz Schlick, Ludwig Wittgenstein, and other logical positivists claimed that religious language is, strictly speaking, meaningless. Others have argued that various divine attributes, such as omnipotence and perfect goodness, are logically inconsistent with one another. And yet others have argued that theism is meaningless. Now, most scholars reject Wittgenstein's ideas about the philosophy of religious language. The idea that God's properties are mutually incompatible often depends on rather specific conceptions of, say, omniscience and omnipotence. And most scholars consider the idea that theism is meaningless to be a relic of logical positivism, which is an outdated view in the philosophy of science.[4] As far as I can see, there's not much to be learned from these arguments. Even more importantly, others have dealt with them in so much detail that I could only repeat them. Such arguments are best treated in analytic-philosophical journal articles.[5] Here, we'll have a look at the more-challenging arguments for atheism, arguments from which both believers and nonbelievers can actually benefit.

The Inefficacy of Prayer

A well-known argument for atheism is that God doesn't respond to prayer. The Abrahamic religions believe in an omniscient, perfectly good, and omnipotent God who listens to the intercessory prayers

---

[4] See also Graham Oppy, "Arguments for Atheism," in *The Oxford Handbook of Atheism*, ed. Stephen Bullivant and Michael Ruse (Oxford: Oxford University Press, 2013), 53–70.

[5] I myself do so, for instance, in "Is Omniscience Impossible?," *Religious Studies* 49, no. 4 (2013): 481–490.

of humans and responds to them, for instance, by healing someone from cancer. The idea here is that this notion of an intervening God is refuted by systematic-prayer experiments. Although a lesser god of some kind might still exist, God as traditionally conceived in religious practices should be given up.

Dozens of such studies have been carried out, and some scientists have even performed a metastudy on these studies.[6] One of the most influential studies that I'll use here by way of example is the study of the therapeutic effects of intercessory prayer (STEP).[7] The purpose of this well-controlled clinical trial was to see whether receiving intercessory prayer was associated with uncomplicated recovery after coronary artery bypass graft surgery. Patients at six US hospitals were randomly assigned to one of three groups, each consisting of roughly 600 patients. One group received intercessory prayer after being informed that they may or may not receive prayer. The second group did not receive intercessory prayer, also after being informed that they may or may not receive prayer. And the third group received intercessory prayer after being informed they would receive such prayer. Here are the results: in the two groups uncertain about receiving intercessory prayer, complications occurred in 52 percent of the patients who received intercessory prayer, in 51 percent of those who did not, and in 59 percent of the patients certain of receiving intercessory prayer. The study concluded that intercessory prayer itself had no effect on complication-free recovery from the surgery but that, remarkably, certainty of receiving intercessory prayer was associated with a higher incidence of complications.

---

[6] See, for instance, David R. Hodge, "A Systematic Review of the Empirical Literature on Intercessory Prayer," *Research on Social Work Practice* 17, no. 2 (2007): 174–187.

[7] See Herbert Benson, Jeffery A. Dusek, Jane B. Sherwood, Peter Lam, Charles F. Bethea, William Carpenter, Sidney Levitsky, Peter C. Hill, Donald W. Clem Jr., Manoj K. Jain, David Drumel, Stephen L. Kopecky, Paul S. Mueller, Dean Marek, Sue Rollins, and Patricia L. Hibberd, "Study of the Therapeutic Effects of Intercessory Prayer STEP in Cardiac Bypass Patients: A Multicenter Randomized Trial of Uncertainty and Certainty of Receiving Intercessory Prayer," *American Heart Journal* 151, no. 4 (2006): 934–942.

Atheists have argued on the basis of such experiments that a God who listens to our prayers, apparently, does not exist. However, there are other ways to interpret the argument. First, one could say that the argument is utterly simplistic. A single element from the many complex practices of prayer – namely, the idea that God responds to prayer – is flattened when we interpret God's response to prayer as God doing exactly what we pray for. It's taken from its original context and transported into the laboratory, and then said to be disproven. This doesn't do justice to the many layers and complexities of prayer.

A second and slightly more charitable interpretation is that this argument disproves a particular, naive conception of what prayer is and what it is for. It can, thus, serve to develop a more mature understanding of the nature and purpose of prayer. Here are a couple of things such a mature understanding of prayer would comprise.

The attitude of faith one has toward God is not the attitude one has toward something mechanical. Take a coffee machine. Its primary purpose is to get you coffee – preferably relatively good coffee. If it doesn't serve that purpose, you have the machine repaired, or you get rid of it. The coffee machine is entirely instrumental to you: you have and keep it only insofar as it gets you your cappuccino. The attitude of faith is not at all like that. Religious believers have the attitude of faith primarily because it arises in response to what they take to be God. God is the perfectly good and loving creator of the universe. That is more than enough reason to believe in him and to worship him, no matter exactly what he gives to us when we ask him for something.

This idea wasn't developed in response to these challenges based on scientific experiments. Rather, it is part and parcel of the Christian faith and, indeed, of religious faith generally. Consider what Augustine wrote already in the fifth century toward the end of a long letter to Proba, a Roman noblewoman and widow of reputedly the richest man in the Roman empire, who wanted to know how best to pray:

> Think over all this, and if the Lord gives you any other idea on this matter, which either has not occurred to me or would be too long

for me to explain, strive in your prayer to overcome this world, pray in hope, pray with faith and love, pray insistently and submissively, pray like the widow in the parable of Christ.[8]

In the thirteenth century, Thomas Aquinas, in his magnum opus *Summa theologiae*, replied in a similar fashion to the question of whether prayer is meritorious:

> Now prayer, like any other virtuous act, is efficacious in meriting, because it proceeds from *charity* as its root, the proper object of which is the eternal good that we merit to enjoy. Yet prayer proceeds from charity through the medium of religion, of which prayer is an act …, and with the concurrence of other virtues requisite for the goodness of prayer, viz. *humility* and *faith*. For the offering of prayer itself to God belongs to religion, while the desire for the thing that we pray to be accomplished belongs to charity. Faith is necessary in reference to God to Whom we pray; that is, we need to believe that we can obtain from Him what we seek. Humility is necessary on the part of the person praying, because he recognizes his neediness. Devotion too is necessary: but this belongs to religion, for it is its first act and a necessary condition of all its secondary acts.[9]

If Augustine and Aquinas are right, prayer requires at least charity, humility, and faith. Thus, for prayer, one's situation, one's history, and one's complex emotional, cognitive, and conative states (one's desires) in relation to God matter. This rules out the potential validity of any experiment in which people are randomly selected to pray, particularly if some of them don't even believe in God.

It's also common knowledge in religious traditions that God can respond to prayer in a multitude of ways, tuned to your unique situation. God can give you exactly what you ask for when you ask it,

---

[8] St. Augustine of Hippo, "Letter to Proba," in *Letters* (Washington, DC: Catholic University of America, 1953), 2:399.

[9] St. Thomas Aquinas, *Summa theologiae*, vol. 3, *1543–1544* (New York: Benziger Brothers, 1948), II.II., q. 83, art. 15. Italics are mine.

God can console you, God can withdraw and hide himself, God can urge you to change your ways, God can invite patience and waiting. Prayer isn't the sort of thing that has predictive power. We pray, and then it's up to God to decide what to do with it.

Moreover, God is not some kind of inert material object that one can use for experimental purposes. In Christianity, Judaism, and Islam, God is the creator of the entire universe. He does not depend on anything else for his existence – he's omnipotent and omniscient, far beyond our understanding. From a religious point of view, it's utterly ridiculous to think we could capture God's actions in a scientific experiment that is meant to definitively establish whether or not God exists.

Thus, the STEP experiment and many others like it encourage us to develop a richer and more mature image of God and a more nuanced understanding of the nature and purpose of prayer.

Belief in God Is a Failing Hypothesis

Belief in God is a hypothesis that fails. Or, slightly more precisely, the hypothesis that God exists fails. It does so for many reasons. Maybe the most important one is that it's just superfluous: we don't need to posit the existence of God or any other deity to explain anything. Everything that needs an explanation can be explained by appealing to entirely natural phenomena. What makes matters even worse is that the God hypothesis has no predictive power, it's not consistent with what we know, and it has no explanatory power. It fails in pretty much every way a hypothesis could possibly fail.

This whole argument strikes me as remarkable. I know virtually no Christians – except maybe for one or two philosophers – who use the word *hypothesis* for their belief in God, let alone for specifically Christian beliefs. There are hundreds of millions of Christians, and they never consider their own religious beliefs as hypotheses – so why should we think of them along those lines? In fact, in everyday life, people hardly ever use the word *hypothesis*. It's clearly an academic word. In university research, we formulate and rigorously test hypotheses. And maybe we do so in a few other highly professionalized scenarios, such as a murder investigation or a large-scale journalistic inquiry. Normal life simply isn't like that. You don't embrace the hypothesis that your partner loves you. You don't work with the hypothesis that female circumcision is morally wrong – it is of course wrong, but this is not a hypothesis. And your belief that you have certain plans for this summer doesn't count as a hypothesis either.

The remarkable thing here is that authors like Richard Dawkins just assume that belief in God is a hypothesis and then go on to argue that the hypothesis fails. They simply don't address the rather obvious preliminary question of why we should think that belief in God is a hypothesis at all.

Atheists who don't pursue this objection to belief in God are perfectly aware that it's misleading to treat belief in God as a hypothesis. According to John Gray, for instance, "religion is an attempt to find meaning in events, not a theory that tries to explain the universe.... The idea that religion consists of a bunch of discredited theories is itself a discredited theory – a relic of nineteenth-century philosophy of Positivism.... The primitive character of the new atheism shows itself in the notion that religions are erroneous hypotheses."[10]

Gray is right. Religious believers don't believe in God as a hypothesis or theory. Rather, for most people it's a basic belief, as we defined it earlier: it's not based on a series of arguments but grounded in intuition and experience. And, as we saw, that can be perfectly fine – many of our beliefs are completely rational even if they are not at all based on arguments. To be sure, analytic philosophers of religion have sometimes treated theism as a hypothesis; for instance, in order to explore whether theism provides a better explanation than

[10] See John Gray, *Seven Types of Atheism* (London: Penguin Books, 2018), 3, 9, 11.

naturalism of such things as cosmic fine-tuning, the fact that there are material things at all, human consciousness, miracles, religious experience, and the fact that beliefs have content. But we should distinguish treating something as a hypothesis in fairly isolated academic debates and for specific purposes from something's actually being a hypothesis. There is something shallow about belief in God that is merely based on the fact that the existence of God is supposed to be the best explanation of certain things.

You Can't Solve Moral Problems by Looking Them Up in the Bible

Another objection that atheists level against religious faith is that a religious person solves moral problems by looking things up in the Bible or some other religious book. But morality doesn't work that way: you can't solve a problem by simply looking for the right answer in a religious text. Also, religious people tend to think we can solve moral challenges only if we consult holy scriptures, but this overlooks the entire, flourishing fields of ethics in which numerous alternatives have been developed. Says Dawkins: "Various schools of moral philosophers, called deontologists, believe you can justify rules on grounds other than simply looking up statements in a holy book."[11]

He is, of course, right that there are plenty of deontologists in the world. In fact, most utilitarians and virtue theorists – the other two big schools in ethics – aren't particularly fond of consulting holy scriptures either. Yet, it's interesting to see how Dawkins portrays the situation: religious believers come to ethical judgments by consulting holy scriptures, whereas secular thinkers use their own minds, formulating general principles and then reasoning through their implications in specific scenarios. An example would be Immanuel Kant's categorical imperative, which says that you

---

[11] Richard Dawkins, *Outgrowing God: A Beginner's Guide* (London: Bantam, 2019), 138.

should always act in accordance with a maxim whereby you can also will that it become a universal law – roughly: treat others as you want to be treated yourself. Another example would be Kant's principle that one should never treat other human beings merely as a means but always as an aim in themselves.

There are indeed religious believers who form their moral opinions merely by consulting holy scriptures, often basing those views on a literal, historical reading of pretty much any text they encounter in those books. Yet, this is characteristic only of a small, fundamentalist minority; it is not how the vast majority of religious believers form their moral opinions. They use moral reasoning, emotional subconscious intuition, tradition, general principles, private feelings, the advice of moral experts, and a nuanced interpretation of larger bodies of passages from, say, the Bible taken together. Particularly for complex moral questions, they seek a balance between these, a so-called reflective equilibrium. Sometimes they embrace a position that is found in the Bible, sometimes they reject a position found there, and sometimes they conclude that their interpretation of a biblical passage must be faulty. In fact, many religious believers are themselves deontologists, utilitarians, or virtue theorists. Faith, then, is surely not a matter of just looking up the answer to complex moral questions in your holy scriptures. Faith means that in complex moral deliberations, one takes the wisdom and inspiration of those scriptures into account, besides much else.

Divine Revelation Would Look Rather Different

According to most religions, God has revealed himself in one way or another. This is certainly true on Christianity, Judaism, and Islam. Such alleged revelation took place in the acts and deeds of prophets and in the books of holy scriptures. However, if these were truly revelations, some atheists reason, they would have looked rather different. They would have revealed things that nobody could have known at the time. Says Sam Harris about prophecies:

> But just imagine how breathtakingly specific a work of prophecy would be, if it were actually the product of omniscience. If the Bible were such a book, it would make perfectly accurate predictions about human events. You would expect it to contain a passage such as "In the latter half of the twentieth century, humankind will develop a globally linked system of computers – the principles of which I set forth in Leviticus – and this system shall be called the Internet." The Bible contains nothing like this. In fact, it does not contain a single sentence that could not have been written by a man or woman living in the first century. This should trouble you.[12]

In the same vein, Dawkins explains what we should expect from Jesus if he were truly divinely inspired:

> Imagine how impressed we'd be if Jesus had told his disciples that the Earth orbits the sun, that all living creatures are cousins, that the Earth is billions of years old, that the map of the world changes over millions of years … But no, his wisdom, impressive though it was in many ways, was the wisdom of a good man in his time, not a god. Just a man, though a good one.[13]

The idea here seems to be that if Jesus had been God, he would've revealed astronomical or biological knowledge or some other cluster of facts about the world that people couldn't have known in some natural way. If that had happened, we would've had decisive evidence for the New Testament being the word of God.

Now, what this argument could equally well show is that, apparently, it was not God's purpose in revealing himself to confer all sorts of scientific knowledge. God, if he exists and is truly omniscient and omnipotent, could easily have informed us about

---

[12] Sam Harris, *Letter to a Christian Nation* (London: Bantam, 2007), 60.
[13] Dawkins, *Outgrowing God*, 121.

big bang cosmology, quantum theory, and evolution long before humans discovered these things themselves. God would've had to work on the conceptual repertoire of first-century Jews and Greeks, but, given his omnipotence, that seems an obstacle that could've been overcome. So, although he could have given people such scientific knowledge, God apparently chose not to do so. Nor was it God's intention to communicate information about other things that seem even more important: how to stop global climate change, how to find a vaccine for COVID-19, how to construe and defend human rights, and how to combat fake news.

Apparently, God wanted to reveal something else. In fact, this is exactly what the main religions say. God wanted to reveal his goodness, his grace, his love, his intentions for humankind, his kingdom, his redemption in Jesus Christ, and the like, not a body of scientific or political knowledge. Christianity has always stressed that God left it to humans to explore the world and to gradually come to know and understand it. Various historians, such as Peter Harrison, have shown in great detail that this has always been a core idea in Christianity and that it shaped the birth of modern universities.[14]

Yet, it's important to stress this, for within some religious groups, fundamentalist minorities have indeed taken God's purpose to also be the conveyance of natural scientific knowledge – about the origin of the cosmos, the origin of human life, anatomy, and hygiene. These truths are thought to be hidden in the Old and New Testaments. Dutch creationist Ben Hobrink's book *Modern Science in the Bible: Amazing Scientific Truths Found in Ancient Texts* nicely illustrates what goes wrong if one takes the purpose of the Bible to be divine communication of scientific truths. Such widely popular books show that, even though this is a minority

---

[14] See Peter Harrison, *The Bible, Protestantism, and the Rise of Natural Science* (Cambridge: Cambridge University Press, 1998); *The Fall of Man and the Foundations of Science* (Cambridge: Cambridge University Press, 2007).

position in religions, it's an influential misguiding force that needs to be taken seriously and time and again proven to be wrong. Arguments by such atheists as Sam Harris confirm how much this is needed. Faith is not a matter of seeking scientific information in holy scriptures – it is a matter of meeting God and distinguishing his voice in these texts.

God of the Gaps

According to the God-of-the-gaps argument, one shouldn't believe in God just because there's something that we can't explain by appeal to natural phenomena. To go supernatural in such a case and base one's belief in God on a gap in our knowledge is a bad move, because such gaps will in all likelihood sooner or later be filled by new scientific discoveries.

The phrase "God of the gaps" was introduced by the Scottish Christian evangelist, biologist, and writer Henry Drummond, who accused his fellow believers as follows in his book *The Ascent of Man*:

> There are reverent minds who ceaselessly scan the fields of Nature and the books of Science in search of gaps – gaps which they will fill up with God. As if God lived in gaps! What view of Nature or of Truth is theirs whose interest in Science is not in what it can explain, but in what it cannot, whose quest is ignorance, not knowledge, whose daily dread is that the cloud may lift, and who, as darkness melts from this field or that, begin to tremble for the place of his abode?[15]

Remarkably, then, the very idea of a God of the gaps was not invented by atheists but by a religious believer who himself considered a God

---

[15] Henry Drummond, *The Ascent of Man* (New York: Cosimo Classics, 2007), 333. First published 1894 by James Pott (New York).

of the gaps to be highly problematic. In any case, the argument in its atheistic version gained prominence when it was leveled against the new creationism of intelligent design, which claimed that there are irreducible complexities in nature that neo-Darwinian evolution cannot explain, such as the bacterial flagellum. Here is what Dawkins says in reply to such claims:

> Searching for particular examples of irreducible complexity is a fundamentally unscientific way to proceed: a special case of arguing from present ignorance…. Creationists eagerly seek a gap in present-day knowledge and understanding. If an apparent gap is found, it is *assumed* that God, by default, must fill it…. Admissions of ignorance and temporary mystification are vital to good science. It is therefore unfortunate, to say the least, that the main strategy of creation propagandists is the negative one of seeking out gaps in scientific knowledge and claiming to fill them with "intelligent design" by default.[16]

Michael Shermer generalizes the point when he says that any appeal to gaps in our knowledge that God is supposed to fill is a God-of-the-gaps argument:

> Cosmologists who find God in the anthropic principle are both theists and naturalists. Supernatural simply means a lack of knowledge about the natural. We might as well call it *ignatural*. To medieval Europeans the weather was caused by supernatural forces; they abandoned that belief when natural forces were understood. This is, once again, the "God of the Gaps" argument, which is what philosophers call "arguments from ignorance." The rules of logical reasoning do not allow the following: "You cannot explain X, therefore Y must be the cause," or, to cut to the chase, "Science cannot explain all life, therefore God must be the cause."[17]

---

[16] Richard Dawkins, *The God Delusion* (London: Bantam, 2006), 151–152.

[17] Michael Shermer, *How We Believe: Science, Skepticism, and the Search for God* (New York: Henry Holt, 2003), 115.

There's a lot to be said about such atheistic criticisms of arguments for God's existence. For one thing, most traditional arguments for the existence of God are not concerned with just any gaps. They have to do with what you could call *gaps that are thought to be principled*. By that I mean gaps that cannot be filled by science because the issue is beyond the purview of science. What proponents of such arguments have in mind are such things as the fact that there are things in the first place, the big bang, the fine-tuning of the universe, human consciousness, beauty, and the regularity of nature. Science, for instance, cannot study the cause of the big bang. If the big bang brought about the universe literally out of nothing (*ex nihilo*), as many cosmologists nowadays believe, then science cannot study the cause of the big bang, since science only studies physical phenomena.

Here, I'd like to draw attention to what we can learn from this argument. What it shows is that one should be rather careful to base one's belief in God on gaps in our scientific knowledge, for these may well be filled sooner or later. I take this to be the main problem with so-called intelligent design, which argues that alleged irreducible complexity, such as that found in the human eye and the bacterial flagellum, is best explained in terms of an intelligent designer. One shouldn't base one's belief in God on arguments that vaporize as soon as a physical explanation is found – and many have argued that it has already been found.

The idea that we shouldn't base belief in God on gaps in our scientific knowledge is in fact one that we find time and again in various religious traditions. Take the German theologian and resistance fighter Dietrich Bonhoeffer. In 1945, he was in prison for involvement in an attempt to take Hitler's life, for which he would eventually be executed. While in prison, he wrote the following on the God of the gaps:

> Weizsäcker's book on the world view of physics is still keeping me busy. It has again brought home to me quite clearly how wrong it is

to use God as a stop-gap for the incompleteness of our knowledge. If in fact the frontiers of knowledge are being pushed further and further back (and that is bound to be the case), then God is being pushed back with them, and is therefore continually in retreat. We are to find God in what we know, not in what we don't know; God wants us to realize his presence, not in unsolved problems but in those that are solved.[18]

This is a remarkable passage, because Bonhoeffer phrases this worry long before the God-of-the-gaps argument was discussed in the literature. Fresh theology has a natural resistance toward basing belief in God on gaps in what we know.

After the Second World War, this became a rather common approach in the science-and-religion discourse. Take what applied mathematician and devout Methodist Charles Coulson says in his *Science and Christian Belief*:

There is no "God of the gaps" to take over at those strategic places where science fails; and the reason is that gaps of this sort have the unpreventable habit of shrinking.... Either God is in the whole of Nature, with no gaps, or He's not there at all.[19]

Religious scientists usually follow this route of avoiding God-of-the-gaps arguments. The BioLogos Institute, which represents numerous Christian academics, answers the question of whether gaps in scientific knowledge are evidence for God as follows:

God-of-the-gaps arguments use gaps in scientific explanation as indicators, or even proof, of God's action and therefore of God's existence. Such arguments propose divine acts in place of natural, scientific causes for phenomena that science cannot yet explain. The assumption is that if science cannot explain how something

---

[18] Dietrich Bonhoeffer, *Letters and Papers from Prison*, ed. Eberhard Bethge (London: SCM Press, 1971), 311.
[19] Charles Alfred Coulson, *Science and Christian Belief* (Oxford: Oxford University Press, 1958), 32, 35.

happened, then God must be the explanation. But the danger of using a God-of-the-gaps argument for the action or existence of God is that it lacks the foresight of future scientific discoveries. With the continuing advancement of science, God-of-the-gaps explanations often get replaced by natural mechanisms. Therefore, when such arguments are used as apologetic tools, scientific research can unnecessarily be placed at odds with belief in God.[20]

Influential figures in the institute, like Francis Collins, actually defend various arguments for God's existence, such as the fine-tuning argument, but they are careful to avoid any God-of-the-gaps arguments.[21]

Thus, this argument could also be interpreted as an encouragement to base one's belief in God on a more solid and more diverse foundation than a series of arguments for God's existence. Apologists who are so into theistic arguments that they consciously or tacitly think that belief in God stands or falls with such arguments miss something crucial. Among the many other potential bases for belief in God are intuitions, personal religious and mystical experiences, communal practices, tradition, making sense of things, testimony of friends and family, liturgy, and divine revelation. I'd submit that in many cases, there may not even be a clear ground. It is not at all uncommon for belief in God to spontaneously arise without there being any clear basis. In such cases, people can't really find a further ground for why they believe in God: it's just the orientation and deep conviction they find themselves with. Atheistic criticisms of God-of-the-gaps-arguments, then, encourage religious believers to develop a richer and more mature faith with a solid basis.

[20] See "Are Gaps in Scientific Knowledge Evidence for God?," *BioLogos*, January 19, 2019, https://biologos.org/common-questions/are-gaps-in-scientific-knowledge-evidence-for-god.
[21] See Francis S. Collins, *The Language of God: A Scientist Presents Evidence for Belief* (New York: Free Press, 2006).

The Smarter, the Less Religious?

A final and rather challenging argument often leveled by atheists against belief in God is that the smarter someone is, the less religious.[22] Here's an example from Alex Rosenberg's *Atheist's Guide to Reality*:

> An unblinking scientific worldview requires atheism. That's why 75 percent of the members of the National Academy of Sciences admit to being atheists. Four-fifths of the rest say they're agnostics – no opinion either way. It can't be a coincidence that 95 percent of the most distinguished scientists in America (along with their foreign associate members) don't believe in God.[23]

This argument easily impresses. If you're even a little bit like me, you'll strongly prefer to belong to the smarter group. But exactly how is it supposed to count against God's existence? Is it indeed true that the smarter you are, the less religious you are? And does that somehow count against belief in God? If it doesn't, how come scientists are less religious than nonscientists?

Let's start with the facts. Scientists or academics in general are indeed less often religious than nonscientists. Nobel Prize winners are hardly ever religious. Some 64 percent of scientists in the United States consider themselves atheistic or agnostic, against an average of 6 percent of the population as a whole.[24] In my own country, the Netherlands, 44 percent of scientists consider themselves atheists, while this is true for only 14 percent of the population at large. Even

---

[22] What follows in this section is based on a Dutch blog that I co-authored with a friend and colleague: Stefan Paas and Rik Peels, "Waarom geloven zo weinig wetenschappers in God?" [Why do so few academics believe in God?], *Geloof&wetenschap*, September 12, 2013, https://geloofenwetenschap.nl/waarom-geloven-zo-weinig-wetenschappers-in-god/.

[23] See Alex Rosenberg, *The Atheist's Guide to Reality: Enjoying Life without Illusions* (New York: W. W. Norton, 2011), viii.

[24] See Elaine Howard Ecklund, *Science vs. Religion: What Do Scientists Really Believe?* (New York: Oxford University Press, 2010), 16–32.

if religion is widespread among the general population, religious belief is significantly rarer among scientists.[25]

Now, can we explain why academics are less religious than people on average? The first thing to note is that it shouldn't be that surprising if we find significantly fewer religious people in one professional occupation than in another. After all, religiosity differs widely among all sorts of categories. Men are on average less religious than women. People living in cities are on average less religious than those living in rural areas. People in Western Europe are on average less religious than people in the United States, and the latter are on average less religious than Africans. The Dutch are less religious than the Italians. Academics are less religious than nonacademics. Sure – so what?

The American sociologist Elaine Howard Ecklund has conducted extensive studies among academics on why many of them are less religious than the average population.[26] Scholars cite such reasons as bad or even traumatic experiences with religion, the problem of suffering, simply being disinterested, and not being raised in a religious way. This matches what we saw when we explored the motivations for atheism. I hasten to add that it's not always easy to identify what truly motivates someone when it comes to the biggest things in life, such as the choice of a spouse or a worldview. The problem, though, is that we find each of these factors among nonacademics as well. Everybody can be irreligious or atheistic for these reasons. So, if we rephrase the issue, the question is this: How come these factors apparently have more impact on scholars than on people in general?

Part of the answer may have to do with self-selection and gender bias in academia. Apart from these factors, though, it is natural

[25] See Martine van Veelen, ed., *Geloof in de wetenschap* [Faith in academia] (Amsterdam: Buijten & Schipperheijn, 2011).

[26] See, for instance, Elaine Howard Ecklund, David R. Johnson, Brandon Vaidyanathan, Kirstin R. W. Matthews, Steven W. Lewis, Robert A. Thomson Jr., and Di Di, *Secularity and Science: What Scientists around the World Really Think about Religion* (Oxford: Oxford University Press, 2019).

to consider those things that all academics have in common and that distinguish them from the average nonacademic, namely, high intelligence, high education, and the academic professional practice. Let us look at each of these.

A few years ago, American psychologists Miron Zuckerman, Jordan Silberman, and Judith A. Hall carried out a careful metastudy on 63 other studies, dating from 1928 to 2012, which explore the relationship between intelligence and religiosity.[27] The researchers defined *intelligence* as the "capacity to reason, plan, solve problems, think abstractly, understand complex ideas, learn quickly and learn from experience." In 53 studies, there was a slight but significant negative correlation between intelligence and religiosity. In other words, the more intelligent people were, the less religious. Since academics are generally intelligent people, one might explain the fact that so few of them are religious by appealing to their intelligence.

Yet, a few caveats are in order. Many of these studies noted this connection among adults. Among younger people – people under 17 – there is hardly any such connection at all. So, intelligence cannot be the only explanation for lower religiosity. The social environment is an explanatory factor as well.

Also, this research has been carried out primarily in the United States. It considered just a few studies from other Western countries, and only two from Europe. No studies from non-Western countries were included. It's not clear, therefore, whether culture plays a role in the relationship between religiosity and intelligence.

Moreover, the researchers only paid attention to a particular kind of intelligence, namely, that which can be expressed in terms of IQ: analytic intelligence. This kind of intelligence is a fairly good predictor of how well one will do in school. Yet, it tells us little about other things. Besides being good at solving mathematical problems,

---

[27] See Miron Zuckerman, Jordan Silberman, and Judith A. Hall, "The Relation between Intelligence and Religiosity: A Meta-analysis and Some Proposed Explanations," *Personality and Social Psychology Review* 17, no. 4 (2013): 325–354.

one can also be really good at resolving social conflicts or at making beautiful art. For this reason, many psychologists nowadays distinguish, in addition to analytic intelligence, creative, practical, emotional, cultural, and social intelligence. It's thus rather simplistic to say that "intelligent people" are less religious.

Finally, there's reason to think that analytic intelligence under certain circumstances contributes to the erosion of the religious sense. Recent cognitive science suggests we have two brain "systems": one that approaches reality intuitively and one that does so more analytically. In other words, we have an intuition to trust someone, to engage in a situation in which someone is in need, or to commit to a relationship, but we also have an inclination to step back and reason our way through a complex problem. We need both systems, but they don't always cooperate harmoniously.[28] Moreover, it seems that generally, people who rely more on their intuitive system more often believe in God.[29] Working from the insights gained from this metastudy, Will Gervais and Ara Norenzayan scrutinized to what extent these cognitive systems can be influenced by specific tasks. They concluded that stimulating the analytic cognitive capacities of test subjects leads to lowered receptivity toward religious belief.[30]

---

[28] Jonathan St. B. T. Evans, "In Two Minds: Dual-Process Accounts of Reasoning," *Trends in Cognitive Sciences* 7, no. 10 (2003): 454–459.

[29] See Amitai Shenhav, David G. Rand, and Joshua D. Greene, "Divine Intuition: Cognitive Style Influences Belief in God," *Journal of Experimental Psychology* 141, no. 3 (2012): 423–428.

[30] See Will M. Gervais and Ara Norenzayan, "Analytic Thinking Promotes Religious Disbelief," *Science* 336, no. 6080 (2012): 493–496. We should note that the study itself isn't at all unproblematic. For one thing, in one of the tests, subjects were presented with texts that contained such words as *analytic, consider,* and *calculate.* After reading texts like these, subjects were less inclined to religious belief than subjects who had looked at texts with more intuitive notions such as *feel, dream,* and *imagine.* There are alternative ways to interpret what's going on here, though. It's possible that analytic notions activated certain cultural prejudices against religion rather than activating the analytic cognitive system. If someone believes or fears that religion doesn't square well with thinking, then that's often not an analytic rational verdict but an intuitive, emotional prejudice. Someone who is

Moreover, the notion of religious belief in these kinds of surveys often boils down to rather primitive and rudimentary naive ideas about spirits, supernatural powers, and ghosts. Research indicates that analytic intelligence does play a role in religions, namely, when believers critically evaluate religious ideas, without actually giving up belief in God.[31] Systematic theology, apologetics, and philosophy of religion are disciplines in which analytic intelligence even plays a pivotal role.

Thus, there's good reason to think that people who rely on a particular cognitive style are generally less susceptible to religious belief. Moreover, meticulous training of our analytic cognitive system over the course of many years and a continuous suspicion toward our intuitive system can erode a potential religious sense and even lead to the abandonment of religious faith. This could well explain, at least in part, why academics are often less religious than other people. Scientific practice can be in tension with religious belief, not because scientific results would conflict with religious faith but because scientific practice leads to a permanent one-sided activation of our cognitive system. Academics are much like professional sports players: they uninterruptedly train certain skills that they have. While this enables them to deliver outstanding performances, it also makes them vulnerable to injuries.

There's a strong connection between the level of education and the degree of religiosity. In general, it's true that the higher one's education, the less religious one is. This is especially true in

---

vulnerable to such things, like almost all of us are, can turn out less religious in a specific test due to the activation of such prejudices. It's true in general that the way we form and express our beliefs depends to some extent on the company or context we are in. In general, we're more convinced of our beliefs in the company of people who share our convictions, and we're more on our guard among people who are critical of our beliefs. It is exactly this sense of being on your guard that can be activated in a study like this.

[31] Thus Gordon Pennycook, James Allan Cheyne, Paul Seli, Derek J. Koehler, and Jonathan A. Fugelsang, "Analytic Cognitive Style Predicts Religious and Paranormal Belief," *Cognition* 123, no. 3 (2012): 335–346.

countries that are highly religious. In more-secularized countries, the connection is much weaker.[32]

Why is it that people with higher education are generally less religious? One might be tempted to posit a rather straightforward explanation: the more someone uses her mind, the more critical she'll be toward religion. Such an explanation is hardly convincing, though. Research shows that education shapes one not only intellectually but also socially, emotionally, and culturally. The values championed in schools are often those of the cultural elite of society.[33] Since the Western elites in particular – both in Europe and in North America – are traditionally rather liberal, it isn't surprising that higher education inculcates secular values in students. Those who receive higher education tend to orient themselves upward: they look to the values that promise social success. That people who are more highly educated are less often religious therefore doesn't have to result from their intellectual and critical thinking but can well be an adaption to the values of the social elite.

Moreover, education tends to select not merely for talent but also for social provenance. In all countries worldwide, kids from the cultural elites reach a higher level of education than children from lower social milieus. Since secular attitudes are better represented among the social elites, this means that people with little religious background have a higher chance of making it into higher education. Education, therefore, tends to reproduce and possibly reinforce existing differences in societies. This is also shown by comparisons between the worldviews of children from the same family. Differences in the level of education among children from the same family can hardly predict how these children will develop

---

[32] See Egbert Ribberink, Peter Achterberg, and Dick Houtman, "Deprivatization of Disbelief? Non-religiosity and Anti-religiosity in 14 Western European Countries," *Politics and Religion* 6 (2013): 101–120.

[33] This is argued by Herbert H. Hyman and Charles R. Wright, *Education's Lasting Influence on Values* (Chicago: University of Chicago Press, 1979).

themselves politically and religiously. But a family's social-cultural circumstances are a good predictor of the family members' worldview, no matter the differences in education.

Both social-cultural provenance and the desire to adapt will impact academics. They will more often come from secular families. After all, secular circumstances tend to reproduce via education. They also will more often adapt themselves to the values of the social elite. They are ambitious people who understandably seek to rise on the social ladder.

Is there also something in the daily work of academics that undermines religiosity? That wouldn't be that surprising. After all, academics are still less religious than intelligent and highly educated people in general. What could explain that?

Well, if you start working in academia, your social environment becomes more one-sided, less diverse. Imagine you finished your secondary school as more or less a religious person and are currently building up your career in the university. From that moment onward, you will increasingly become part of a population that is largely nonreligious. Since human beings are social beings, there will be significant pressure from your peers to adapt yourself to these new circumstances. Moreover, a serious academic career demands enormous amounts of time and energy. Those who reach the summit will have little time for other things, let alone for frequent Bible reading, daily prayer, and going to church on a weekly basis. Also, having an academic career means using your analytic cognitive system even more intensively. Growing specialization and workload, which will enhance insensitivity toward religious questions and beliefs, will do the rest. An academic work environment is also highly competitive and ambitious. These values are rather in tension with religious ones like humility and love for your neighbor. People can diminish this tension by taking things easy in their academic career or simply by not even starting it. But they can also just give up religion or never set out to live as a religious person.

Finally, as Zuckerman points out, intelligent people often have more success in life.[34] They have better jobs, make more money, are healthier and more prosperous, have more often a partner, and have a higher sense of dignity. In short, they don't need the advantages offered by religious faith – things like community and empowerment – as much as others do. Academics, especially the ones who excel, generally meet these criteria.

That academics are less religious is thus best explained by a combination of different factors. Social and cultural backgrounds play a role, as well as stimulating a particular type of intelligence in a specific social environment over a longer period of time. People who choose an academic career, it seems, will end up in a secularizing "perfect storm." This raises another interesting question, one that we can't answer here but that fascinates me: How should we think of the people who remain or even become religious while having a flourishing academic career? Nobel Prize–winning Egyptian American chemist Ahmed Hassan Zewail (1946–2016) is known as the father of femtochemistry, the field that studies chemical reactions on extremely short timescales. Yet, he was also a Muslim who explained on many occasions that he saw no conflict between science and belief in God. Francis Collins is the former leader of the Human Genome Project and former director of the National Institutes of Health. Yet, he is also a devout Christian and an avid apologist. How do such people manage to combine these things?

It's time to draw a lesson from this argument against belief in God. The argument shows something that many religious people have been aware of all along, but it's useful to be reminded of it. Being a person of faith is not a matter of being intellectual, clever, smart, or scientific. Thus, your intelligence or academic profile says nothing about your sensitivity toward or insight into

---

[34] See Zuckerman, Silberman, and Hall, "The Relation between Intelligence and Religiosity," 346.

God's existence and his relationship with humans. Of course, faith involves your mind, but it's not a matter of being clever. Rather, it's a matter of your soul – your self and your innermost motivations in life – being tuned toward the divine.

What Atheism Tells Us about Religious Faith

Let's wrap up. We've seen that there is much value in many atheistic arguments. An important insight that can be gleaned from some of these arguments is that faith in God is not like belief in a theory or a hypothesis. It's a complex affective, cognitive, and conative state of mind and orientation of life. It has to do with the aim of living and interpreting one's life and the lives of others in the light of God. Being a person of faith is not a matter of being smart, let alone of being smarter than others. Of course, it involves one's mind as well – Christ himself said to his followers: "Love the Lord your God with all your heart and with all your soul and with all your mind."[35] But it's much more than that: it's opening yourself up to the grace of God's reality in your life. For religious believers, God's existence is not a hypothesis that is more plausible than its rivals, but an experienced reality that they devote themselves to in worship and adoration. If you are a person of faith, you probably believe in God as a person. God is similar to us, because he is a person and the God who made the physical reality we live in. But God is also radically different from us, because he is God and we are humans. God is far beyond is in goodness, grace, and wisdom. We are fallible and finite beings. God may respond to our prayers, but sometimes he doesn't, for reasons we often don't know. Even if he does, he may do so in a multitude of ways. Only in some cases do we receive what we pray for. To be a person of faith is to believe in God, to trust God, to commit your life to God, to seek to serve

---

[35] Matt. 22:37.

and honor God. Other religions also acknowledge God or several gods; religious believers are normally fully aware of that. Persons of faith usually don't believe that all other religions are radically misguided. Rather, they have experienced the truth and value of God as thought of in their own religion. What matters is whether one actually *worships* God. Other religions are presumably right on some matters and mistaken on others.

6 | Atheistic Arguments and God

God's Lack of Efficiency

Let's now turn to atheistic arguments that might tell us something about God. An important idea among atheists is that there can't be a creator God because nature is remarkably inefficient at times. Any human designer would do a better job. Says Richard Dawkins:

> It will have occurred to you that there's a problem with lying on your side if you're a fish.... So, what did the plaice and flounders do about it? They grew a distorted, twisted skull, so that both eyes look upwards instead of one being flat against the sea bottom. And I do mean twisted and distorted.... No sensible designer would have produced an arrangement like that. It makes no sense from a design point of view, but it has history written all over its Picasso-like face.[1]

Being an avid sea fisher myself, I've got to admit that, on the contrary, I find the twisted and distorted Picasso-like face of plaice, flounders, halibut, and the like rather beautiful. But maybe Dawkins is right that there may be more efficient ways to have both eyes on one side of the body than having them migrate sometime between the larval and juvenile stages. Sam Harris similarly thinks that what we see is just utterly inefficient if God created the earth:

> Over 99 percent of the species that ever walked, flew, or slithered upon this earth are now extinct. This fact alone appears to rule out

---

[1] Richard Dawkins, *Outgrowing God: A Beginner's Guide* (London: Bantam, 2019), 164.

intelligent design. When we look at the natural word, we see extraordinary complexity, but we do not see optimal design. We see redundancy, regressions, and unnecessary complications; we see bewildering inefficiencies that result in suffering and death. We see flightless birds and snakes with pelvises. We see species of fish, salamanders, and crustaceans that have nonfunctional eyes, because they continued to evolve in darkness for millions of years. We see whales that produce teeth during fetal development, only to reabsorb them as adults. Such features of our world are utterly mysterious if God created all species of life on earth "intelligently"; none of them are perplexing in light of evolution.[2]

The idea is that blind evolution, with its inefficiency and waste, is a much more plausible explanation for numerous inefficient processes than divine creation.

Of course, this argument works only if we add certain assumptions about the intentions of God the creator. A perfectly good God, so the idea seems to be, would never use a detour but always go for the most efficient way, and he would create things directly rather than via a long, complicated process. Thus, in putting forward this argument, Dawkins, Harris, and others are not really engaging in biology or physics. They are turning themselves into amateur theologians, working with rather explicit ideas about God's purposes and intentions.

Now, do those ideas match what the main religions say about God's intentions? I think they don't. True, on mainstream Christianity, God at some point decides to create humans and numerous animals. But God also has many other intentions; for example, to create things of beauty, to bring into existence things of goodness, to make creation relatively autonomous, and to create things that are vast on a scale of time and place so that the universe displays God's greatness. God didn't create the world

---

[2] Sam Harris, *Letter to a Christian Nation* (London: Bantam, 2007), 75.

in order to constantly intervene; he made a universe that is ruled by regularities and that displays the gradual enfolding of biodiversity. Also, God may well have further intentions that partially conflict with the previous ones, which means he has to balance his goals. God may have the intention, for instance, to make his existence not too obvious, so that having faith in a loving and caring God is still a free choice.

Remarkably, the ideas that Dawkins and Harris advocate about God's intentions fit much better with Christian fundamentalism, creationism in particular. In most versions of creationism, God made all the biological species directly through a series of creative acts. A more charitable reading of the argument from inefficiency is to say that God would never use a long evolutionary process of waste but would create things in a splendid and perfect state directly, very much like creationism says God did. Only, Dawkins and Harris's conclusion is the opposite: rather than giving up on evolution, they give up on God.[3] They share the basic conception of God's intentions in creation with the creationist. A natural way to read this argument, then, is that it shows the creationist – and Dawkins and Harris's – image of God's intentions in creation to be too simple and misguided. In creating things, God has a wide variety of purposes that may even partially conflict with each other, so that he has to balance them. Moreover, mainstream religions would stress that we can know only some of his intentions. Other intentions of God may remain hidden to us. Mainstream Christianity would encourage modesty and humility when it comes to our ability to map God's intentions in creation. So, the argument from inefficiency helps us to have a more nuanced view of God's intentions.

---

[3] As philosophers like to say, one person's *modus ponens* is another person's *modus tollens*. In other words, it can happen that two people share the premise "if *p*, then *q*," but the one adds "*p*, and therefore *q*," whereas the other adds "not-*q*, and therefore not-*p*."

Russell's Teapot

The teapot argument was first introduced by British philosopher Bertrand Russell:

> Many orthodox people speak as though it were the business of scep-
> tics to disprove received dogmas rather than of dogmatists to prove
> them. This is, of course, a mistake. If I were to suggest that between
> the Earth and Mars there is a china teapot revolving about the sun
> in an elliptical orbit, nobody would be able to disprove my asser-
> tion provided I were careful to add that the teapot is too small to be
> revealed even by our most powerful telescopes. But if I were to go
> on to say that, since my assertion cannot be disproved, it is intoler-
> able presumption on the part of human reason to doubt it, I should
> rightly be thought to be talking nonsense. If, however, the existence
> of such a teapot were affirmed in ancient books, taught as the sacred
> truth every Sunday, and instilled into the minds of children at school,
> hesitation to believe in its existence would become a mark of eccen-
> tricity and entitle the doubter to the attentions of the psychiatrist in
> an enlightened age or of the Inquisitor in an earlier time.[4]

The New Atheists have picked up this argument and extended it. Says Dawkins:

> In some strict sense we should all be "teapot agnostics." In practice
> we are a-teapotists. You can be an atheist in the same (technically
> agnostic) way you're an a-teapotist, an a-fairyist, an a-pixieist, an
> a-unicornist, an a-anything-you-might-dream-up-ist.[5]

This argument says belief in God is very much like belief in a teapot that orbits the sun and is invisible to telescopes. Since we have
no evidence for it whatsoever, we shouldn't believe in it. A simple

---

[4] Bertrand Russel, "Is There a God?," in *The Collected Papers of Bertrand Russell*, ed. John G. Slater, vol. 11, *Last Philosophical Testament, 1943–1968* (Oxford: Routledge, 1952), 542–548.

[5] Dawkins, *Outgrowing God*, 13.

point that's overlooked by Russell and Dawkins, however, is that this wouldn't justify atheism in the stronger sense that there is no God – it would, at most, justify agnosticism. Naturally, I agree it's only sensible to believe there's no teapot orbiting the sun. But that's because we have much relevant background knowledge. For example, it is excessively unlikely that this teapot would have spontaneously come into existence. Therefore, someone would have had to bring it into existence and then put it into an orbit around the sun. This is extremely unlikely. In order for this to be a sound argument for atheism, we'd also need much background evidence that would render the existence of God highly unlikely. Most atheists haven't provided such evidence; they simply suggest that belief in God is as ridiculous as belief in a china teapot that orbits the sun. The rhetoric here is considerably stronger than the argumentative force.

Yet, there's plenty that this atheistic argument can teach us. God, if he exists, is not at all like a china teapot. He isn't an entity in the physical whole of space-time, whereas teapots are, as are tables, chairs, cities, swamps, mountains, planets, iPhones, black holes, even quantum fields. You would expect this to be obvious, for the main monotheistic traditions have stressed time and again that God is the creator of the physical universe and, therefore, not a part of it. Some theologians, such as Paul Tillich, even speak of God as the "ground of being."[6] Yet, various atheists seem to have trouble grasping this. According to Graham Oppy, "it is clear that, if there is an omniscient, omnipotent, and perfectly good being running our universe, then that being is a denizen of our universe and occupies a particular location within in."[7] I find it hard to understand how he came to embrace this somewhat idiosyncratic view of God that doesn't seem to match what Judaism, Christianity, and Islam actually tell us about God.

---

[6] See Paul Tillich, *Systematic Theology* (Chicago: University of Chicago Press, 1951), 1:235.

[7] See Graham Oppy, "What I Believe," in *50 Voices of Disbelief: Why We Are Atheists*, ed. Russell Blackford and Udo Schüklenk (Oxford: Wiley-Blackwell, 2009), 51.

Not only is God not an entity in the universe, but God is also not remotely like any other entity, not even like other entities that are beyond the universe. Many abstract objects, such as properties, propositions, universals, and numbers, are not in the universe. They are immaterial objects, as philosophers, logicians, and mathematicians would stress. Yet, these are all *abstract* objects: they can't bring anything about. So, God is unlike them in that he has causal powers. In fact, he is thought to be omnipotent: he can do anything. Most importantly, God is thought to be in some sense the *fons et origo* of everything. In other words, he is the source and creator of all things that exist – at least the material things but, according to some, also the immaterial things. As the Nicene Creed has it: "I believe in one God, the Father Almighty, Creator of heaven and earth, of all things visible and invisible." A teapot orbiting the sun does not in any way affect one's worldview. A personal God who has created everything that exists and continues to interact with our world, on the other hand, has ramifications for pretty much *anything* in one's worldview.

Another crucial difference is that God, unlike a teapot or any other material object, is a person. A teapot orbiting the sun probably won't try to get in touch with you. And should you get in touch with it, interaction or mutual affection isn't to be expected. If God is a person, then it seems not at all unlikely that he reveals himself in various ways, that he responds to our concerns and praise, and that he has plans and intentions and acts on them. To pursue the teapot argument is to miss out on what should be obvious: God is in no way like a material object in the universe. He is the very creator of the universe, not a part of it.

Who Created God?

Speaking of God as creator, if God created the earth, the universe, life on earth, biological complexity, humans, consciousness, and even good and evil, then who created God? Does God's existence explain anything at all, or do the important questions just move up one level? Doesn't belief in God push around a bulge under the carpet rather than just stomping it out entirely? Here's how Daniel Dennett ridicules the idea of a creator God:

> Children chant, "It takes one to know one," but an even more persuasive slogan would seem to be "It takes a greater one to make a lesser one." Any view inspired by this slogan immediately faces an embarrassing question, however, as Hume had noted: If God created and designed all these wonderful things, who created God? Supergod? And who created Supergod? Superdupergod? Or did God create Himself? Was it hard work? Did it take time? Don't ask! Well, then, we may ask instead whether this bland embrace of mystery is any improvement over just denying the principle that intelligence (or design) must spring from Intelligence. Darwin offered an explanatory path that actually honoured Paley's insight: real work went into designing this watch, and work isn't free.[8]

It is unclear to me why Dennett here doesn't go into a simple idea constitutive of all major monotheistic religions, namely, that God is radically unlike his creation. Creation is contingent. In other words, it exists, but it could have failed to exist. God, however, is not like that. God exists necessarily – that is, he *has* to exist. Creation has not always been around, for the universe is some 13.8 billion years old. God, on the other hand, is eternal (beyond time) or at least everlasting: he has always existed and will always exist. The created world was brought into existence by an external cause, namely, God, whereas God is *a se* (not dependent on anything else). He was not brought into existence by anything or anyone, not even by himself. That's what religions, particularly monotheistic ones, have been saying for centuries.

---

[8] Daniel C. Dennett, *Darwin's Dangerous Idea: Evolution and the Meanings of Life* (New York: Simon & Schuster, 1995), 71.

The Argument from Scale

Human life has existed for 200,000 years. That may sound like a lot, but the universe is actually some 13.8 billion years old. That means that humans have been around for less than 0.002 percent of the universe's history. If that isn't already impressive, take the size of the universe. There are around 100 billion planets in our galaxy, and there are probably around 200 billion galaxies in the observable universe. Out of those countless planets, we inhabit exactly one. If there had been a God who values human life, it would've been abundant in both time and space. But there is hardly anything of it. Therefore, there cannot be a God who cares much about human life.

This line of reasoning is known as the argument from scale. In fact, there is a whole host of arguments from scale with slight variations. Famous American skeptic and science writer Michael Shermer is succinct but clear:

> Why would a deity make a universe that is 13.7 billion light years in radius, in which practically none of it is usable? It is just a waste of stuff. Why would a deity do that?[9]

The hinge of Shermer's argument is the uselessness of so much matter. Sean Carroll, famous for his contributions to cosmology, is more elaborate on this idea:

> There are many features of the laws of nature which don't seem delicately adjusted at all, but seem completely irrelevant to the existence of life. In a cosmological context, the most obvious example is the sheer vastness of the universe; it would hardly seem necessary to make so many galaxies just so that life could arise on a single planet around a single star. But to me a more pointed observation is the existence of "generations" of elementary particles. All of the ordinary matter in the universe seems to be made out of two types of quarks (up and

---

[9] See the introductory video by Michael Shermer, executive director of the Skeptics Society, at www.thegodquestion.tv.

down) and two types of leptons (electrons and electron neutrinos), as well as the various force-carrying particles. But this pattern of quarks and leptons is repeated threefold: the up and down quarks are joined by four more types, just as the electron and its neutrino are joined by two electron-type particles and two more neutrinos. As far as life is concerned, these particles are completely superfluous. All of the processes we observe in the everyday workings of the universe would go on in essentially the same way if those particles didn't exist. Why do the constituents of nature exhibit this pointless duplication, if the laws of nature were constructed with life in mind?[10]

Carroll isn't claiming that lots of the universe's space and matter is just useless, but he observes that much of it is irrelevant, particularly *for the existence of life*. For him, the amount of redundant empty space counts against the idea that our universe is tailored toward the emergence of intelligent life. Nicholas Everitt uses the famous phrase "jewel of creation" in his version of the argument:

For something more than 99.999 per cent of the history of the universe, the very creatures which are meant to be the jewel of creation have been absent from it…. Assuming that the expansion was at less than the speed of light, that still leaves the possibility of a universe whose overall size is between 10 and 30 billion light years across (i.e. up to two million trillion miles). Why would a God make it that big? … What could be the point of the huge superabundance of celestial matter, especially given the fact that the very great majority of humanity will never be aware of most of it? Again, given the theistic hypothesis, it is strikingly inapt.[11]

In my view, it's not so much the superabundance of celestial matter that's inapt as the idea that God wanted humankind to be the jewel

[10] Sean M. Carroll, "Why (Almost All) Cosmologists Are Atheists," *Faith and Philosophy* 22, no. 5 (2005): 633.

[11] Nicholas Everitt, *The Non-existence of God* (London: Routledge, 2004), 216–217. For yet another version of the argument, see Herman Philipse, *God in the Age of Science? A Critique of Religious Reason* (Oxford: Oxford University Press, 2012), 312.

of creation. This idea conflicts with the age and size of the universe. If God had wanted us to be the jewel of creation, he would have created ... well, what would he have created? Maybe something like the cozy universe that the first chapters of Genesis describe on a literalist reading: not too big, fairly transparent to the human intellect, in line with the human time span, with humans at the center and some – but not too many – celestial decorations. But this is not at all what we find.

Many technical questions can be raised here about the argument from scale. How can we be sure exactly how much of the universe is hospitable to intelligent life? Do we really know how empty the universe is? One can also raise numerous philosophical questions. For instance, if human beings have value, is it true that the more humans there are, the better? Wouldn't humans have greater value if they were rather unique? And what if humans come to populate large stretches of the universe and the universe will continue to exist for much longer than it has existed so far?

Although these are fascinating questions, I want to zoom in on something else. The primary value of this atheistic argument, I take it, is that it invalidates naive ideas about humans being the jewel of creation. Of course, in Christianity, humankind has a special place in the cosmos. The first few chapters of Genesis describe humans even as the high point of God's creation. Made in the image of God (*imago Dei*), humans take center stage in God's creation. Consider what the sixteenth-century Reformer John Calvin says:

> We ought in the very order of things diligently to contemplate God's fatherly love toward mankind in that he did not create Adam until he had lavished upon the universe all manner of good things. For if he had put him in an earth as yet sterile and empty, if he had given him life before light, he would have seemed to provide insufficiently for his welfare. Now when he disposed the movements of the sun and stars to human uses, filled the earth, waters, and air with living things, and brought forth an abundance of fruits to suffice as foods,

in thus assuming the responsibility of a foreseeing and diligent father of the family he shows his wonderful goodness toward us.[12]

God, according to Calvin, is a caring and diligent father. Before he put humans on earth, he made sure there was enough water and plenty of fruits and animals; he even disposed the movements of the sun and stars to human uses. The rest of the Bible, too, is centrally concerned with God's intentions and plans for humanity. Furthermore, Christianity has always held that one chief reason for God's becoming human was to redeem humankind. In this approach, humans are clearly important in God's plans.

Yet, some Christians have gone much further and claimed that the entirety of the created world centers around human beings. This atheistic argument makes us question whether that is right. Why not think that God, in creating the universe, had many different purposes and that the flourishing of humanity is only one of them?

Perhaps God had aesthetic purposes in mind. It's hard to deny that the Milky Way, the Pleiades, the Andromeda Galaxy, supernovae, and the birth of a star, for example, are a beautiful sight. Maybe God cares especially about human beings, but that doesn't mean he couldn't care nonspecially about many other things. He may not care as much about, say, galaxies, stars, planets, or dark matter as he does about you and me, but he may still find these things important and valuable enough to create them and sustain them in existence for very lengthy periods of time. We humans do similar things. Although we don't care as much about, say, the things we craft as we do about family and friends, we still value these things and are attached to them.

Note that in the first few chapters of Genesis and elsewhere in the Bible, contrary to what most people seem to assume – including Nicholas Everitt and numerous religious believers – humans really aren't the jewel of creation. That honor goes to the seventh day, the Sabbath. This day of rest is not just the cessation from all the hard

---

[12] John Calvin, *Institutes of the Christian Religion*, ed. John T. McNeill (Louisville: Westminster John Knox Press, 1960), 1:161–162. First published 1536.

work but, in a sense, its very culmination and purpose. The creation story in Genesis 1 describes how God works for six days, in order then to celebrate and rejoice in everything he has made. God doesn't make the universe in order for us to live in it, but he makes the entire universe, including us, for himself to enjoy. Of course, God cares about us, and we rejoice in many of the world's things as well, but we should be cautious not to think that creation is really all about us.

Not only might God value nonanimate matter in the forms of such things as planets, stars, and dark matter, but he might also value other phenomena – things that explain why human life is not pervasive in time and space. What I have in mind here are specific events, such as the spontaneous and autonomous development of the cosmos. There might be something good about things developing slowly and gradually in the course of time. We can also think of the cosmos as a whole: it might be good for there to be a certain balance between chaos and order.

In fact, God may have numerous other purposes, ones that we cannot even fathom since we know so little about the cosmos, let alone about reality as a whole – material and immaterial alike. We already saw that mainstream religions like Christianity rightly draw our attention to our cognitive limits: we know so little about the universe that it is wise to be modest about our capacities to independently estimate what God's purposes and intentions are or could be.[13]

Let me be clear that Christians should frankly admit the church has sometimes fallen into the trap of thinking that God is really primarily concerned with human beings. As many historians of science have argued, the shock that came for theologians in the fifteenth and early sixteenth centuries when Nicolaus Copernicus, Giordano Bruno, and Galileo Galilei adduced all the evidence for heliocentrism was not that the earth isn't flat – they had known that for centuries – but

---

[13] Stephen Wykstra, "The Humean Obstacle to Evidential Arguments from Suffering: On Avoiding the Evils of 'Appearance,'" *International Journal for Philosophy of Religion* 16 (1984): 73–94.

that the earth is not the center of the universe (in other words, that geocentricism is false). We are in the periphery. We matter less than we thought. Or maybe we just found that we hadn't been accorded the place we would have given ourselves if we could.

The awareness that, while humans are special, God has created a vast universe was already present among the ancient Israelites. Take this contemplation by the author of Psalm 8:

> When I consider your heavens,
>   the work of your fingers,
> the moon and the stars,
>   which you have set in place,
> what is mankind that you are mindful of them,
>   human beings that you care for them?
> You have made them a little lower than the angels
>   and crowned them with glory and honor.[14]

This atheistic argument, then, rightly calls for humility: human beings are of tremendous value, but hubris shouldn't draw us into thinking that God only cares about humanity. More importantly, it can enrich our understanding of God's nature and character: there's good reason to think that in creating the world, God had countless other purposes in mind besides making humans. Among them were moral and aesthetic purposes that extend to other living beings and, for all we know, even to inanimate matter.

The Problem of Evil

The Swiss theologian Hans Küng rightly called the problem of evil "the rock of atheism."[15] Undoubtedly, it has been the most serious objection to the existence of God. The evil, pain, and suffering in

---

[14] Ps. 8:3–5.
[15] Hans Küng, *On Being a Christian*, trans. Edward Quinn (Garden City: Doubleday, 1976), 432.

this world remain a stumbling block for many religious people. The challenge is that a perfectly good, omnipotent, omniscient God would not allow all the pain, evil, and suffering in the world. Since such evil is clearly there, the only reasonable option is to believe that there is no God. David Hume crisply summarized the problem as follows: "Is he [God] willing to prevent evil, but not able? then is he impotent. Is he able, but not willing? then is he malevolent. Is he both able and willing? whence then is evil?"[16] The problem of evil has found its way into many literary works of art as well. In *The Brothers Karamazov*, Fyodor Dostoyevsky, himself a profoundly religious man, has Ivan tell his brother Alyosha:

> Listen: if everyone has to suffer in order to bring about eternal harmony through that suffering, tell me, please, what have children to do with this? It's quite incomprehensible that they too should have to suffer, that they too should have to pay for harmony by their suffering. Why should they be the grist to someone else's mill, the means of ensuring someone's future harmony? … I absolutely reject that higher harmony. It's not worth one little tear from one single little tortured child…. The price of harmony has been set too high, we can't afford the entrance fee. And that's why I hasten to return my entry ticket. If I ever want to call myself an honest man, I have to hand it back as soon as possible. And that's exactly what I'm doing. It's not that I don't accept God, Alyosha; I'm just, with the utmost respect, handing Him back my ticket.[17]

The problem naturally returns in the writings of the New Atheists. Says Daniel Dennett:

> The idea that God is a worthy recipient of our gratitude for the blessings of life but should not be held accountable for the disasters

[16] David Hume, *Dialogues concerning Natural Religion and Other Writings*, ed. Dorothy Coleman (Cambridge: Cambridge University Press, 2007), 74, part 10, sect. 25. First published 1779 in London.

[17] Fyodor Dostoevsky, *The Brothers Karamazov*, trans. Ignat Avsey (Oxford: Oxford University Press, 1994), 306–308. First published 1879–1880 in *The Russian Messenger*.

is a transparently disingenuous innovation of the theologians....
The Problem of Evil, capital letters and all, is the central enigma con-
fronting theists. There is no solution. Isn't that obvious? All the holy
texts and interpretations that contrive ways of getting around the
problem read like the fine print in a fraudulent contract – and for
the same reason: they are desperate attempts to conceal the implications of the double standard they have invented.[18]

In fact, there's a whole host of problems of evil. Is God's existence logically compatible with evil? Does evil render God's existence improbable? Does the actual amount of evil render God's
existence improbable? Do particular evils render God's existence
improbable? Is God's existence unlikely in the face of moral evil,
such as the Holocaust? Is it unlikely in the face of natural evil,
such as earthquakes and forest fires? How does one as a religious
person deal with all the pain and suffering in this world?

Ever since the rise of the Darwinian theory of evolution, matters
have become even worse for belief in God. To see how, let's first
be a bit more precise on what we mean by *Darwinian evolution*.
Following Paul Draper, one could distinguish between *evolution* on
the one hand and *Darwinism* on the other. The idea of *evolution*,
this American philosopher suggests, consists of two theses. On the
genealogical thesis, all complex organisms are the more or less gradually modified descendants of a small number of simple unicellular
organisms. On the *genetic* thesis, all evolutionary change in pop-
ulations of complex organisms is either identical to or the result
of transgenerational genetic change. *Darwinism* says that natural
selection operating on random genetic mutation is the principal
mechanism driving evolutionary change.[19]

---

[18] Daniel C. Dennett, "Problem of Evil and Religion's Double Standard," *Washington Post*, January 19, 2010.

[19] See Paul Draper, "Evolution and the Problem of Evil," in *Philosophy of Religion: An Anthology*, ed. Louis Pojman and Michael Rea, 7th ed. (Belmont: Wadsworth, 2015), 273. This distinction is also accepted by others; e.g., Daniel Howard-Snyder, "The

The genealogical and genetic theses jointly raise important questions for religious belief. Are humans still unique, let alone created in the image of God, if they are just the descendants of unicellular organisms? Are humans still meant to exist in such a case? What to make of divine providence? How should we interpret the first few chapters of Genesis? Is the evolutionary process compatible with a Fall, or is moral evil part and parcel of the universe? But it is particularly the Darwinist thesis that is important here. For how could a perfectly good and loving God use or even install a process that works by way of natural selection upon random mutation? This process directly implies the suffering, waste, and loss of billions and billions of lives of all living creatures. Ever since the rise of Darwinism, arguments from evil can now draw on extra material, often especially gruesome. Darwin himself phrased this worry in a well-known letter to Asa Gray on May 22, 1860:

> I own that I cannot see, as plainly as others do, and as I should wish to do, evidence of design and beneficence on all sides of us. There seems to me too much misery in the world. I cannot persuade myself that a beneficent and omnipotent God would have designedly created the Ichneumonidae with the express intention of their feeding within the living bodies of caterpillars, or that a cat should play with mice.[20]

It's often overlooked that the problem of evil is particularly unsettling when one embraces a specific image of God, for instance, as we find it among Jews and Christians.[21] God is thought of as someone

Evolutionary Argument for Atheism," in *Being, Freedom, and Method: Themes from the Philosophy of Peter van Inwagen*, ed. John A. Keller (Oxford: Oxford University Press, 2017), 241–262.

[20] Darwin's full correspondence, as far as we know it, can be found on the website of the Darwin Correspondence Project. For this particular letter, see www.darwinproject.ac.uk/letter/?docId=letters/DCP-LETT-2814.xml&query=asa%20gray.

[21] I've written in more detail about these properties of God and their relation to evolution in my "Does Evolution Conflict with God's Character?," *Modern Theology* 34, no. 4 (2018): 544–564. What I say here is based on various ideas developed in that article.

who consistently chooses the side of the weak, the poor, the vulnerable, the outcasts. Of course, there's room for altruism in evolution, and it's not always the strongest who survives, but overall there's a clear conflict: evolution generally prefers the well-adapted, whereas God prefers the widows, the orphans, the weak, the sick, and others who are not well-adapted and whose chances of survival are low.

Already in early Genesis God prefers Abel, whose name literally means "nothingness," over his much stronger brother Cain.[22] God chooses Israel, a tiny and negligible people, over the powers of Egypt and Babylonia.[23] God anoints David as the future king, and not one of his older brothers.[24] God condemns Israel's leaders for not caring for the poor and needy.[25] In the New Testament, God chooses a poor girl to be the mother of Christ.[26] In incarnating, God gives up divine power and status.[27] Christ is born in Bethlehem, not exactly a metropolis.[28] Christ dies on a cross, the fate of criminals.[29] Dutch-American literary scholar and priest Henri Nouwen rightly characterizes Jesus's mission in life as "the selfless way of Christ," a path that leads downward.[30] For those who embrace this picture of God, then, the theory of evolution makes the problem of evil even larger.

The problem of evil has been extensively addressed long before there was substantial atheism on earth. This shows that evil was considered a serious pastoral and intellectual challenge independently of whether it leads some people to reject God's existence. Entire books in the Bible, such as Job and Lamentations, provide theological insight into God and suffering. In fact, it is part and

---

[22] Gen. 4:4–5.

[23] Deut. 7:7–9.

[24] 1 Sam. 16.

[25] Jer. 22:16, Hosea 5:14–24.

[26] Luke 1:48.

[27] Phil. 2.

[28] Matt. 2:1.

[29] 2 Cor. 13:4.

[30] Henri Nouwen, *The Selfless Way of Christ: Downward Mobility and the Spiritual Life* (New York: Orbis Books, 2007).

parcel of the Christian liturgy not only to think about God and suffering but to actually address and invoke God himself as the only one who can truly help us in our deepest need. From Hildegard von Bingen's "Kyrieleison" to Johann Sebastian Bach's "Erbarme dich, mein Gott," the problem of evil is a pervasive phenomenon in the life of the religious believer – not primarily as something that is supposed to question God's existence, but as something that urges us to seek God.

Nowadays, in our secular societies in which the problem of evil makes many question the very existence of God, we find a wide array of theories, suggestions, and solutions – or at least partial solutions – to various problems of evil. Some provide a defense, aiming to show the logical compatibility of God and evil. Others give a theodicy (from the Greek *theos*, "God," and *dikè*, "justice"), that is, an attempt to show that the existence of evil is not even unlikely if God exists. Such theodicies invoke the idea that such greater goods as mercy, compassion, consolation, bravery, and many other things would be impossible without the existence of evil and suffering. They appeal to the order and regularity of nature and refer to our inability to oversee history and the hidden purposes or by-effects that evil events may have. Even the evil acts of demons and other fallen angels have been considered in explaining the evil in this world.

A reply that has been particularly influential is the *free-will defense*. The basic idea is that there is enormous value to our having free will. Without it, we would bear no responsibility, and we might not even be persons at all. However, free will inevitably comes with the possibility of misusing it in order to do evil. This point can be brought out by drawing on Darwinian evolution. If natural processes selected the sick, poor, and weak, it would only be natural that people cared for them. They would, in a sense, be hardwired to do so. We, however, live in a world in which Darwinian processes rule, and those processes haven't left us untouched: we are naturally inclined to fight for ourselves and our kin rather than for strangers, for those in need. It often really takes a conscious effort to do good, to be merciful, to care for those with little social status.

In his movie *The Tree of Life* (2011), director Terrence Malick seems to have exactly this in mind when Mrs. O'Brien, one of the main characters, says:

> The nuns taught us there are two ways through life: the way of nature and the way of grace. You have to choose which one you'll follow. Grace doesn't try to please itself. Accepts being slighted, forgotten, disliked. Accepts insults and injuries. Nature only wants to please itself. Get others to please it, too. Likes to lord it over them. To have its own way. It finds reasons to be unhappy when all the world is shining around it, when love is smiling through all things.

A reply along these lines raises many further questions. To be sure, free will is worth much, but can it justify, say, the Shoah or the terror famine in Ukraine known as the Holodomor that killed some five million people? Couldn't God at least sometimes intervene? What about all the suffering that has nothing to do with the choices made by humans? Does free will really require that one can do evil – isn't God free, for instance? I've addressed such questions elsewhere.[31] But let me be frank that I do believe that the problem of evil remains the largest and most profound challenge for anyone who believes in God. It may even provide serious evidence against God's existence. If that's the case, then whether one can rationally believe in God will, obviously, also depend on the evidence *for* God's existence.

Here, I'd like to make a different point: there's much to be learned from this argument, particularly by religious believers. For one thing, belief in God is utterly untenable on a certain image of God. If your theology is that God's primary purpose is to give all humans the most pleasant or happiest lives they could imagine, then your belief in God is indeed in trouble. If God is fully aware of

---

[31] See Stefan Paas and Rik Peels, *God bewijzen: Argumenten voor en tegen geloven* [Why it's OK to believe in God] (Amsterdam: Balans, 2013).

all the suffering and is perfectly able to stop it, then why wouldn't he do so if his purpose is just to make us as healthy, comfortable, and happy as possible? The idea that God's ultimate purpose is the wealth, health, and happiness of humankind is not that far-fetched. It's the core of the rather popular *prosperity theology*. Here's what revivalist preacher Gordon Lindsay says about wealth and health:

> Wealth is produced through industry. Sick people are unable to work, or at least to work effectively. As a result many, because of illness, are in poverty. But God has promised health for the Christian. Even under the law, the obedient believer was promised deliverance from sickness.[32]

Even more explicit is Israeli Christian televangelist Benny Hinn:

> Sickness does not belong to you. It has no part in the Body of Christ. Sickness does not belong to any of us. The Bible declares if the Word of God is in our life, there will be health, there will be healing – divine health and divine healing. There will be no sickness for the saint of God. If Moses could live such a healthy life, so can you.[33]

What alternative image of God is suggested by the problem of evil? A much more complicated picture, on which many of God's purposes and intentions are hidden to us. An image on which God seems harsh, merciless, or even cruel at times. An image on which, with Job, one will have to say about God:

> Though I cry, "Violence!" I get no response;
> though I call for help, there is no justice.
> He has blocked my way so I cannot pass;
> he has shrouded my paths in darkness.
> He has stripped me of my honor
> and removed the crown from my head.

[32] Gordon Lindsay, *God's Master Key to Prosperity* (Dallas: Christ for the Nations, 2001), 114.
[33] Benny Hinn, *"Rise and Be Healed!"* (Orlando: Celebration Publishers, 1991), 15.

> He tears me down on every side till I am gone;
>   he uproots my hope like a tree.
> His anger burns against me;
>   he counts me among his enemies.
> His troops advance in force;
>   they build a siege ramp against me
>   and encamp around my tent.[34]

On this image, God is sometimes present with his grace, mercy, and beauty, but at other times he seems against us, as in Job's case. Life can be unforgivably cruel. Atheists, agnostics, and religious believers alike don't always get a response to their prayers and cries. In some cases, the believer has an idea of God's intentions and purposes, but in other cases, she has no clue whatsoever. The believer's own moral depravity and self-deception can stand in the way, but very often, that's not the case. Any serious religious image of God will have to do justice to that.

The Problem of Divine Hiddenness

There's another, closely related argument against God's existence that I consider to be really challenging: the problem of divine hiddenness. It is in many ways similar to the problem of evil. Proponents of the argument from divine hiddenness point to a negative feature of the world that they find hard to reconcile with a perfectly good, omnipotent God, particularly God as portrayed in Christianity. They have in mind God's hiddenness. Friedrich Nietzsche is his usual eloquent self when he asks:

> A god who is all-knowing and all-powerful and who does not even make sure that his creatures understand his intention – could that be a god of goodness? Who allows countless doubts and dubieties to

---

[34] Job 19:7–12.

persist, for thousands of years, as though the salvation of mankind were unaffected by them … ? Would he not be a cruel god if he possessed the truth and could behold mankind miserably tormenting itself over the truth?[35]

John Schellenberg put the issue on the contemporary philosophical agenda more than anyone else. This Canadian philosopher rigorously conceptualized the argument from divine hiddenness. What makes the argument so appealing is that, from the very outset, it is inspired not just by mere theism but by specifically Christian ideas about God. He sets out with an analogy:

> Imagine yourself in the following situation. You're a child playing hide-and-seek with your mother in the woods. You've been hiding for some time now behind a tree. It appears to be quite the hiding place but not impossible to discover, but she does not appear. It's now getting dark and it's almost bedtime, but still no mother. Not only isn't she finding you, but, more disconcerting, you can't hear her anywhere: she's not beating the nearby bushes, making those exaggerated "looking for you" noises, and talking to you meanwhile as mothers playing this game usually do. Now imagine that you start calling for her. Coming out from behind the tree, you start yelling, "Mooooommmmm!" But no answer. You look everywhere: through the woods, in the house, down the road. An hour passes, your voice has grown hoarse from calling. Is she anywhere around? Would she fail to answer if she were around?[36]

The idea is clearly that a perfectly good, omnipotent, and omniscient God who created us in his image, loves us, and seeks a relationship with us would not allow this to happen. Maybe an omniscient,

[35] Friedrich Nietzsche, *Daybreak*, ed. Maudemarie Clark and Brian Leiter, trans. R. J. Hollingdale (Cambridge: Cambridge University Press, 1997), 52–53, sect. 91.

[36] John Schellenberg, "Divine Hiddenness Justifies Atheism," in *Contemporary Debates in Philosophy of Religion*, ed. Michael L. Peterson and Raymond J. VanArragon (Oxford: Blackwell, 2004), 31.

omnipotent, perfectly good being would let this happen. But surely not a God with the specific properties ascribed to him in the Christian religion, one who seeks a personal relationship with us. Such a God would provide conclusive evidence for his existence and make sure that everyone experiences his love and presence. Hence, there can't be such a God.

This argument calls for a richer and more profound anthropology and soteriology (theory of salvation) than some religious believers and secular people seem to work with. Clearly, there are similarities between God's relationship to us and our relationship with our children, yet the two are not exactly alike. We might leave our children for a short period of time (we bring them to day care) or maybe even leave them for years in a row in time of war, and we might even bring about suffering on their part (we bring them to the dentist, admonish them if they behave wrongly), but we wouldn't choose to be absent. We would seek to know them and seek for them to know us, even if it took great effort. Although God's relationship to us is in certain ways like the relationship of parents with their children, it is not that kind of relationship. The reason for this is simple: there are structural dissimilarities. God is God: eternal, perfect, almighty, and omniscient. Humans are humans: fallible, evil at times, contingent, finite, and mortal.

What could be the purpose of God in hiding himself? Why would God be silent? In exploring these questions, philosophers and theologians have come up with numerous suggestions. Maybe if God made himself obvious to everyone, we would lose our freedom, somewhat similar to how children behave when their parents are standing in the doorway. And maybe such freedom is of immense value, even if it entails the possibility of performing evil deeds. Another option is that God's hiddenness forms us in certain ways that are good. Particularly, many of us come to seek God, sometimes persistently so. We come to desire justice and truth, beauty and love. We come to long for God's presence. Maybe these things wouldn't be there if God had been obviously present all along. Yet another option is a form of skepticism: we simply don't know what God's purposes are in hiding himself; sometimes, we can't even think of any such purposes. But that's not really surprising, given that we are finite and limited human beings while God is eternal and far beyond us in power and wisdom. Again, the argument draws attention both to the wide variety of purposes that God may have and to our own limitations as human beings.

Note that these responses all draw on ideas from *perfect-being theology*, that is, the idea that there is a perfectly good and omnipotent God. However, the argument from divine hiddenness is particularly poignant for specific religions, and for Christianity perhaps more than for any other. After all, the argument works from the assumption that God seeks a personal loving relationship with humans in the way that parents love their children. But if the argument relies on such theological ideas, it is equally permissible to use such ideas in replying to it. This is exactly what Michael Rea does in a recent response to the argument from divine hiddenness.[37] This American philosopher suggests we should distinguish between communication and communion. One can perfectly well be with someone without verbally communicating. One can have silent communion with someone, for instance, in walking together. Maybe it's part of God's personality, Rea says, that his preferred mode of interaction is silence. One of God's purposes may be to be true to himself. Again, reality doesn't evolve around us. Rea could draw on several Bible passages here. In 1 Kings 19, for example, the prophet Elijah is at Mount Horeb. First, there's a great wind, but God's not in there. Then, there's an earthquake, but God is not to be found in it. Subsequently, there's a fire, but God is absent from it. Finally, there's a sound of sheer silence. That's where Elijah meets God.

I don't think such responses entirely solve the problem. There are all sorts of important follow-up questions to be asked here. For God

---

[37] Michael Rea, "Divine Hiddenness, Divine Silence," in *Philosophy of Religion*, ed. Louis Pojman and Michael Rea, 7th ed. (Belmont: Wadsworth, 2015), 383–392.

does, presumably, reveal himself in a nonsilent way in many other cases. And one may wonder why God would remain silent if speaking is the only way to make some people believe in him. The problem of divine hiddenness remains in many ways a serious obstacle and challenge. Yet, again, I believe that it makes us ask questions about God that can really help us move beyond an image of God that is all too primitive and anthropomorphic. If God were like us, he would reveal himself decisively. But he doesn't. God isn't like us, and he never was. He has purposes of his own, some of which we know, some of which we can fathom, and some of which may be unimaginable for us. This is important not only for atheists and agnostics but equally for religious believers, for they often face divine silence as well. Take what Mother Teresa wrote in one of her letters published posthumously:

> Lord, my God, who am I that You should forsake me? The child of your love – and now become as the most hated one – the one You have thrown away as unwanted – unloved. I call, I cling, I want – and there is no One to answer – no One on Whom I can cling – no, No One. – Alone. The darkness is so dark – and I am alone. – Unwanted, forsaken…. In spite of all – this darkness & emptiness is not as painful as the longing for God. – The contradiction I fear will unbalance me. – What are You doing My God to one so small? When You asked to imprint Your Passion on my heart – is this the answer?[38]

Dealing with or often just bearing temporary and sometimes even permanent divine silence is part of the faith of many religious believers.

Two Worries

If I'm right that the value of many atheistic arguments lies in their call for fine-tuning our belief in God or our ideas about God's nature

---

[38] Mother Teresa, *Come Be My Light: The Private Writings of the Saint of Calcutta*, ed. Brian Kolodiejchuk (New York: Doubleday, 2007), 186–187.

and character, shouldn't we start to worry that religions will always change in the course of time? Wouldn't it follow that Christianity can never be defeated, because religious believers can always take an atheistic argument to count against a particular conception of faith or of God, make the required changes, and then go on believing? Isn't this something like moving the goalposts, or changing the rules during the game? It's a common complaint among atheists that these are all ad hoc refinements, so that religious belief is *guaranteed* to survive any objection leveled against it. Says A. C. Grayling:

> To put the matter graphically, contesting religion is like engaging in a boxing match with jelly: it is a shifting, unclear, amorphous target, which every blow displaces to a new shape. This is in large part because the religious themselves often do not have clear ideas, or much agreement among themselves, about what is meant by "religion," "god," "faith" and associated concepts. And this is not surprising given the fact that these concepts are so elastic, multiple and ill-defined as to make it hard to attach a literal meaning to them.[39]

I don't think we should worry that religions immunize themselves from criticism in this way. On the one hand, the slightly more nuanced, fine-tuned conceptions of faith and of God were not first formulated in response to these objections but have been part and parcel of various holy scriptures and religious practices since long before that. We already saw that the Bible is replete with passages about God's hiddenness. Sometimes he grants a prayer, sometimes he doesn't, and sometimes he grants it in a way one did not ask for. On the other hand, flexibility is usually taken to be a strong point of a view, something that counts in a view's favor. Why would things be any different here? Christianity, for instance, is a worldview, and its holy scriptures are clothed in the historical-cultural circumstances in which they were written down (and revised and edited). We need

---

[39] A. C. Grayling, *The God Argument: The Case against Religion and for Humanism* (London: Bloomsbury, 2013), 4.

theology, science, and such humanities as archaeology and history for understanding the original author-intentional meanings, for knowing the reception or *Wirkungsgeschichte* of the text, and for deciding what the relevant passages can mean for us. It's only natural that science, new developments in theology and philosophy, discoveries in the humanities, and cultural developments, such as new directions in moral awareness, lead to new insights.

Another worry one may have, especially about the picture of God that I sketched, is that if God is so incomprehensible to us, we can no longer know God's intentions. In other words, we would have to become skeptics regarding God's will. We would no longer have any idea of what God aims to do in our lives, in the world, and in the universe. This objection is sometimes raised by atheists, such as Herman Philipse. They point out that if one claims we can't know God's intentions, we can't appeal to them in providing arguments for God's existence either. Says Philipse:

> What reasons can God have had for preferring the long evolutionary route of the history of the cosmos and of life, if he wanted to create the human species? Theists should not answer this question by the traditional bromide that God's intentions are inscrutable for us. Such a move would annihilate the predictive power of theism, and thereby destroy the prospects of natural theology. Instead, they should come up with convincing reasons for God to take the evolutionary detour, assuming that he probably wanted to create humans in the first place.[40]

This is a fair worry. It's part of the systematic theology of several religions that we can know at least some of God's intentions, say, in incarnating in Jesus Christ, in performing various miracles, and in judging the world. Moreover, as Philipse rightly points out, the idea that we can know some of God's intentions plays a crucial role

---

[40] Philipse, *God in the Age of Science?*, 276. The point is also made by Rob Lovering, *God and Evidence: Problems for Theistic Philosophers* (New York: Bloomsbury, 2018), 87–104.

in a number of arguments for God's existence, such as the Islamic *kalam* cosmological argument (it is not at all unlikely that God would intend to create a physical universe), the fine-tuning argument (it is likely that if God creates a physical universe, he would want there to be intelligent life), and the moral argument (it is likely that God would want us to know some important moral truths).

There may be several ways, though, in which religious believers can still claim to know at least some of God's intentions. Certain divine intentions seem to simply follow from mainstream conceptions of God as found in perfect-being theology, which says that God is perfect in all regards. If God is himself a person and he is perfectly good and omnipotent, it doesn't seem at all unlikely that he will create other intellectual beings, other persons. Even if this isn't particularly likely, all that is needed for the argument from fine-tuning is that God's forming this intention is more likely than there being fine-tuning by sheer luck. Moreover, it is widely thought within various religions that God has revealed himself and that among the things he has revealed are some of his plans, decisions, and intentions. In Christianity, God is thought to have a special plan with Israel, to have decided to incarnate and live a human life, and to intend to save humankind, to return, and to redeem and judge the world.

What Atheism Tells Us about God

We've seen that atheistic arguments teach us much about how to construe a tenable, sound, religiously and theologically profound image of God that goes beyond stereotypes. I believe that taking these arguments seriously will lead to a purification of faith, a process in which we get rid of an all-too-anthropomorphic image of God, the God as we would want him to be rather than who he is.

In mainstream Christianity, God is thought to care for humans. Yet, our happiness is not God's sole purpose, and possibly not even his primary purpose. He wants a loving relationship with humans; moreover, he wants human beings to voluntarily enter into that relationship. The world is complex, and only God knows how to accomplish his purposes with humans individually and with humankind in general. This means that there are lots of things in this world we can't explain, such as certain kinds of evil and God's hiddenness at crucial junctures in our lives. Sometimes, later on in our lives, we are able to make sense of them, but more often, our questions remain unanswered. The life of faith in this God is an adventure: it requires trust in God, you have no idea how the journey is going to end, and it involves all your intellectual and emotional strength.

This picture of God is common in somewhat theologically reflective environments. In fact, we can find these ideas already in the holy scriptures of the Old and New Testaments and in other time periods long before these atheistic objections were leveled. These arguments, however, are continuous reminders to stay clear of an all-too-simplistic image of God and to maintain an open mind toward theological nuance and flexibility.

I'm not denying that there are serious disagreements between atheists and religious believers; of course there are. Those disagreements need to be addressed. The arguments need to be rigorously assessed in terms of their logical validity and in terms of the a priori and empirical evidence for each of their premises. But if I'm right, then even if an atheistic argument is discredited, it can still have value: it can lead to a richer, deeper, and more mature understanding of God.

7 | Life after Atheism

Rational Atheism?

We've witnessed how, in many cases, atheism is based on personal motivations, such as the desire to follow an intellectual hero. It can also be grounded in different kinds of cognitive frameworks, like the idea that only science provides knowledge. Some have defended a presumption of atheism, which would make atheism the default position, but we saw that this faces some serious problems. Last but not least, we explored various kinds of atheistic arguments. Many of them don't really provide evidence against belief in God. But virtually all of them draw our attention to important features of religious faith or even of the nature and character of God. There's much to be learned from them, then.

It's hard to deny that, overall, we haven't been able to adduce strong evidence for atheism. Does it follow that atheism is inevitably irrational? No, it doesn't. After all, we also saw that some arguments for atheism are promising and truly hit their target, namely, arguments from evil and arguments from divine hiddenness. These often target belief in God as professed by mainstream religions such as Christianity and Islam. In addition, there are highly technical arguments against belief in God that we couldn't cover in this book. Sometimes, these are just refined and logically formalized versions of arguments that we considered, but there are also complicated arguments in the literature that are really too technical to address in a book like this. Analytic philosophers of religion may base their atheism on such arguments. Of course, whether these arguments render their atheism rational doesn't depend solely on the quality of their arguments. It also depends on the quality of the evidence in favor of God's existence. Here, we can think of versions of the Anselmian ontological argument for God's existence, the cosmological argument, the moral argument, fine-tuning arguments, the argument from religious experience, the argument from miracles, and dozens of others that are increasingly receiving philosophical attention.[1] Maybe it also depends on evidence from testimony, experiential evidence such as transcendent experiences of goodness and beauty, and much more. This book is about atheism, so we haven't delved into these arguments and other kinds of evidence for theism, let alone for any specific religion. What we've seen, then, isn't an answer to the question of whether atheism can sometimes be rational. Maybe it can, maybe it can't.

Yet, what we've seen is truly important. After all, very few people base their atheism on the kind of highly technical philosophical arguments that we find in academic journals in the philosophy of religion. Most atheists base their atheism on personal motivations, general cognitive frameworks like scientism, or the kinds of atheistic arguments that we explored in this book. Or they may just assume the truth of atheism as a default position. This means that in many cases, atheism really is in trouble from an intellectual point of view. Therefore, let's explore where these atheists can go from here.

Agnosticism

A natural response would be to retreat to agnosticism. Agnosticism, after all, suspends judgment on whether or not there's a God.

---

[1] For elaborations of these arguments and further arguments for God's existence, see William Lane Craig and J. P. Moreland, eds., *The Blackwell Companion to Natural Theology* (Oxford: Wiley-Blackwell, 2012); Alvin Plantinga, "Two Dozen or so Good Theistic Arguments," in *Alvin Plantinga*, ed. Deane-Peter Baker (Cambridge: Cambridge University Press, 2007), 203–227.

Maybe there is a God, maybe not – agnosticism isn't committed either way. Some bolder versions assert not only that we don't know whether there is a God but that we cannot possibly know whether there is a God.

Agnosticism is a viable option. Maybe it is exactly the position that's warranted by the evidence that some people have or by their lack of certain kinds of evidence. Maybe their evidence for and against God's existence is balanced. It will comprise the fact that there are sincere testimonies of millions of normal, healthy, intelligent people who say they don't experience God. It will also comprise the fact that there are equally sincere testimonies of millions of other people who claim that they've had religious, transcendent, and mystical experiences. It involves various puzzling features of the universe, such as that it came from nothing, that it is so well-ordered, that life is possible, and that we have consciousness. And it contains serious problems that count in favor of atheism: all the evil and suffering in the world, the fact that people hold such radically divergent beliefs about the transcendent realm, and the chaos and arbitrariness that seem to pervade our lives. I can well imagine that some people are agnostics, and I can't see why that wouldn't be perfectly rational in some cases.

Yet, one might have hesitations about agnosticism. For it's plagued by a pernicious problem: one is guaranteed to miss out on crucially important truths.[2] Either God exists or he doesn't. Either the universe is created or it isn't. Either we are meant to be or we aren't. The agnostic who suspends judgment on the existence of God will, unfortunately, inevitably fail to believe the truth about these issues.

Perhaps it is, as such, not that bad to suspend judgment every now and then. I suspend judgment on the safety of a Russian vaccine that

---

[2] As we already saw, the American psychologist William James famously argued that there are two aims of cognition: to believe the truth and not to believe any falsehoods. To suspend judgment would be not to believe a falsehood, but it would also necessarily miss out on the truth. See William James, *The Will to Believe and Other Essays in Popular Philosophy* (Cambridge, MA: Harvard University Press, 1979), 24.

hasn't yet been tested, I suspend judgment on the details of Shakespeare's life, since we know so little about him, and I suspend judgment on whether the total number of stars in the universe is now even or odd. But here's the point: whether or not God exists is radically unlike such relatively minor things. It's among the most important issues imaginable, or maybe *the* most important issue – and in fact, religious believers and atheists agree on this. Whether or not God exists makes a difference to morality, to our role in this universe, to what the meaning of life is, to whether or not there's an afterlife, to what a good life is, to our ideas about what exists apart from us, and so on. To miss out on the truth about God's existence, then, is also to miss out on countless other crucially important truths.

The agnostic may feel uncomfortable about this. At least, I'd fully understand if she did. Now, maybe that's just the way things are, and we'll have to live with it. But maybe there are other options; let's explore.

Choosing to Believe and Influencing Your Beliefs

One could suggest that, since agnosticism guarantees that one will miss out on the most important truth in life, one should just choose atheism or theism. In other words, one should just choose to believe either that there's no God or that God exists. One may not have enough evidence either way to be sure, but at least one has a decent chance of believing the truth.

The main problem here is that we can't really choose to believe something. I don't mean just atheism – I mean almost anything. Of course, we *say* every now and then – well, I don't, but philosophers may not be representative here – that we choose to believe something. But upon closer inspection, it turns out that we don't really choose our belief in such cases. Rather, what we do is make up our minds, and that results in a belief of a particular kind. Could you, right now, choose to believe that the Roman empire never existed, or that the earth is flat, or that all COVID-19 vaccines are harmful? You may reply that you can't but that that is just because these views are utterly implausible. However, the same holds for more-controversial issues. Could you, just by choice, change your current views on contested moral issues, like euthanasia and abortion, or controversial political issues, such as whether it was legitimate for Russia to invade Ukraine or whether governments should play a role in fighting human-induced climate change? The problem here is that our beliefs and our disbeliefs and our suspensions of judgment follow the evidence we take ourselves to have. We carefully think through the evidence we have, weigh the pros and cons, and then a belief simply *arises* – we don't really *choose* it. We can't just believe by fiat.[3] Philosophers have called this *doxastic involuntarism*: it is involuntary which doxastic attitudes (from the Greek *doxa*, "belief") we have. This view is widely accepted in the literature.[4]

We can't choose to believe, then. But there's much we can do to influence our beliefs, and this is exactly what we do when we make up our minds. In fact, we often properly expect people to exercise precisely such influence. The police can study the evidence at the crime scene and thereby make a difference in what they know about the murder. Public defenders can delve into dossiers on the suspect and in that way influence their beliefs about her. A student can prepare for her exam in marine biology by studying

---

[3] I think there are highly exceptional scenarios in which we can choose to believe; see my "Believing at Will Is Possible," *Australasian Journal of Philosophy* 93, no. 3 (2015): 524–541.

[4] William Alston gave various examples of an inductive argument for doxastic involuntarism. See William P. Alston, "The Deontological Conception of Epistemic Justification," in *Epistemic Justification: Essays in the Theory of Knowledge* (Ithaca: Cornell University Press, 1989), 115–152. See also René van Woudenberg, "Belief Is Involuntary: The Evidence from Thought Experiments and Empirical Psychology," *Discipline Filosofiche* 22 (2012): 111–132. Others, such as Bernard Williams, have given a more conceptual argument for it. Here, the idea is that something wouldn't properly count as a belief if we could choose to hold it. See Bernard A. O. Williams, "Deciding to Believe," in *Problems of the Self: Philosophical Papers 1956–1972* (Cambridge: Cambridge University Press, 1973), 136–151.

the textbook and attending class. Or, to give even more-mundane examples, we can check our agendas to see whether we're right about an appointment, we can listen to someone we disagree with so that we can come to understand her, and we can read the news so that we come to know whether there've been more fires in the Amazon rainforest lately.

When we zoom out a little, there are three kinds of things we can do to influence our beliefs. First, we can improve the mechanisms that produce our beliefs. For instance, we can train our memory, take a course in logic, cultivate our moral sensitivity, or work on our aesthetic sense by taking classes in art history. Clearly, doing so is generally conducive to acquiring beliefs that are more accurate and better founded. Second, we can work on our evidence. We can study files, read dossiers, check the news, do a personal investigation, speak to people. In fact, we should also sometimes intentionally avoid evidence, for instance, when it comes to issues of privacy or decency. Third, we can work on our cognitive virtues and vices. As we saw earlier, these are cognitive character traits that affect what we believe. We can seek to be more open-minded, humbler, more thorough, more creative, or more perseverant.[5] We can try to become less gullible, less narrow-minded, less stubborn, and less superficial. All of that will make a difference in what we believe.

So, what can we do to influence our beliefs about the existence or nonexistence of God? Well, here are some examples of things we can do:

- seek argumentative evidence concerning God's (non)existence, both that provided by atheists and that of religious believers;
- study the mystical and other religious experiences of religious believers;

---

[5] For a more detailed account of how each of these three factors could work, see my *Responsible Belief: A Theory in Ethics and Epistemology* (New York: Oxford University Press, 2017), chap. 3.

- talk to atheists, get to know them, and understand why they are atheists (the same holds for religious believers);
- listen to the life stories of atheists and religious believers;
- study the history of atheism and the histories of several religions;
- get acquainted with religious traditions, rituals, and liturgies; and
- attempt various means to get in touch with God – for instance, prayer and reading holy scriptures – in order to discover things about God's existence and his relation to humanity.

These are cases of influence, not of control. We don't know in advance which beliefs or which faith, secular or religious, we'll end up with. We may maintain our agnosticism; we may find better grounds for being an atheist; we may abandon our suspension and become a person of faith in God. Only time can tell.

Pascal's Wager

So, it looks like we're able to influence our beliefs about God. But do we actually have any reason to do so? Why not just stick to agnosticism and spend our time on other issues?

Purely pragmatic considerations are a good place to start here. Just sticking to agnosticism might make us miss out on things we value, like full happiness, well-being, or *eudaimonia* (in case you have a penchant for Greek philosophy). It's worth quoting Blaise Pascal at length here:

> If there is a God, He is infinitely incomprehensible, since, having neither parts nor limits, He has no affinity to us. We are then incapable of knowing either what He is or if He is….
>
> … "God is, or He is not." But to which side shall we incline? Reason can decide nothing here. There is an infinite chaos which separates us. A game is being played at the extremity of this infinite distance where heads or tails will turn up. What will you wager?

According to reason, you can do neither the one thing nor the other; according to reason, you can defend neither of the propositions.[6]

Pascal suggests, then, that we are in a situation in which we must wager: for or against belief in God. Either we live as if God exists or we live as if he doesn't. How then should we go about this wager? He makes a couple of suggestions:

> Since you must choose, let us see which interests you least. You have two things to lose, the true and the good; and two things to stake, your reason and your will, your knowledge and your happiness; and your nature has two things to shun, error and misery. Your reason is no more shocked in choosing one rather than the other, since you must of necessity choose. This is one point settled. But your happiness? Let us weigh the gain and the loss in wagering that God is. Let us estimate these two chances. If you gain, you gain all; if you lose, you lose nothing. Wager then without hesitation that He is. – "That is very fine. Yes, I must wager; but I may perhaps wager too much." – Let us see. Since there is an equal risk of gain and of loss, if you had only to gain two lives, instead of one, you might still wager. But if there were three lives to gain, you would have to play (since you are under the necessity of playing), and you would be imprudent, when you are forced to play, not to chance your life to gain three at a game where there is an equal risk of loss and gain. But there is an eternity of life and happiness. And this being so, if there were an infinity of chances, of which one only would be for you, you would still be right in wagering one to win two, and you would act stupidly, being obliged to play, by refusing to stake one life against three at a game in which out of an infinity of chances there is one for you, if there were an infinity of an infinitely happy life to gain. But there is here an infinity of an infinitely happy life to gain, a chance

[6] Blaise Pascal, *Thoughts*, trans. W. F. Trotter, in *Thoughts and Minor Works*, The Harvard Classics, vol. 48 (New York: Collier, 1910), 84, sect. 3, n. 233.

of gain against a finite number of chances of loss, and what you stake is finite.[7]

So, Pascal's idea is that we stand to gain infinitely by living as if God exists if God does indeed exist, whereas we lose little by living such a life if there is no God. Note that Pascal doesn't say we ought to believe that there's a God. Rather, in what follows, he advises us to act as if we believe: by going to church, attending mass, reading holy scriptures, praying, going to confession, and so on. These are all actions that might give us access to evidence about God's existence and thus indirectly bring about belief in God. His suggestions, then, square perfectly well with what we've seen so far: we can't choose to believe in God or not to believe in God, but we can choose to do numerous things that make a difference to whether or not we believe in God. In fact, Pascal rather explicitly rejects doxastic voluntarism. We can't believe at will. Yet, we can influence what we believe:

> At least learn your inability to believe, since reason brings you to this, and yet you cannot believe. Endeavour then to convince yourself, not by increase of proofs of God, but by the abatement of your passions. You would like to attain faith, and do not know the way; you would like to cure yourself of unbelief, and ask the remedy for it. Learn of those who have been bound like you, and who now stake all their possessions. These are people who know the way which you would follow, and who are cured of an ill of which you would be cured. Follow the way by which they began; by acting as if they believe, taking the holy water, having masses said, etc. Even this will naturally make you believe, and deaden your acuteness. – "But this is what I am afraid of." – And why? What have you to lose?[8]

My point here is not whether Pascal's wager is a sound pragmatic argument for trying to bring about belief in God. My fellow philosophers

---

[7] Pascal, *Thoughts*, 85, sect. 3, n. 233.

[8] Pascal, *Thoughts*, 86, sect. 3, n. 233.

have already discussed that extensively.[9] Rather, my point here is that, according to Pascal, we have good practical reason to seek evidence for God and, thus, to exercise influence over belief in God. If, indeed, God exists, happiness, well-being, and *eudaimonia* are to be found both in this life and in the afterlife only in a personal relationship with the God who created us and wanted us to exist. It makes perfect sense, therefore, to think that we should seek evidence concerning the existence of God rather than staying content with being an agnostic.

In fact, this point also holds for belief that there's no God. If there's no God, then there may be a certain happiness in realizing that, or it may be part of the good life to be aware of that and see what follows from it for our morality, the place of humans in the cosmos, and so on. Clearly, things are complicated here. Some philosophers of religion have argued that if there's no God, there are no objective moral values, there's no meaning to life, and even intentions and consciousness are illusions. If they are right about that, then that may well have implications for how much happiness and well-being can be had on atheism. But of course, all that is debatable. Perhaps the most reasonable thing to conclude here is that there's only one way to find out: by delving into all the evidence, both theoretical and practical, for and against God's existence. The proof of the pudding is in the eating. No matter how one thinks of Pascal's wager, he is undoubtedly right that, whenever possible, we should not remain content with agnosticism but do our utmost to find all the evidence that bears on God's existence.

Moral and Intellectual Reasons

However, pragmatics can't be the whole story. For there are also moral considerations. Imagine that God exists. Wouldn't we then

[9] See, for instance, Elizabeth Jackson and Andrew Rogers, "Salvaging Pascal's Wager," *Philosophia Christi* 21, no. 1 (2019): 59–84.

be wronging someone if we failed to find out whether or not God exists – namely, God himself? Compare it to a situation in which you have lost a family member. They may still be alive or they may not be alive; you just don't know. If you're not sure, though, you have a moral duty to search for them. Of course, God isn't our family. Yet on mainstream Christianity, Judaism, and Islam, God has created humans – possibly even in his own image. Therefore, we should try to find out whether God exists and, if so, who he is. If we fail to do so, in being disinterested we would wrong him, not just practically but also morally.

Things are a little less clear if atheism is true. If God doesn't exist, then we probably wouldn't be wronging anyone if we failed to find out whether or not God exists. Surely, we wouldn't be wronging God. Maybe we would owe it to ourselves or to humanity, though, given the enormous theoretical and practical ramifications of whether or not we believe in God.

But even this is not the whole story. There are also purely intellectual considerations, or, as philosophers like to call them, purely epistemic reasons – reasons that have to do with truth and falsehood, with knowledge and understanding. Of course, we can't be obligated to seek out just any truth whatsoever. We can't be expected to study every tree in the Siberian forests or every snowflake in Antarctica. There are literally endless amounts of truths about this world, and we can't possibly study each of them – thankfully!

Yet, belief in God is different. Truths are hierarchical in the sense that some of them are more important than others. Let me give an example from biology. Truths about mutations in an individual wombat are subordinate to truths about mutations in the population to which that wombat belongs. The latter are less important than truths about developments in mammals. Those latter are subordinate to truths about mutations in animals. They, in turn, are not as important as truths about mutations in living organisms. And the latter are trumped by evolutionary explanations of biodiversity in general. Now, I can't be expected to hold true beliefs about various specific wombats. There are just too many such truths in the world, and they aren't particularly important. But I do have a good reason to learn at least the basics about evolutionary theory, given its far-reaching implications and the public accessibility of evidence for evolutionary theory. Arguably, something similar applies to the basics of history, arithmetic, literature and other arts, chemistry, and astronomy: as human beings, especially those with ample education, we need to know the basics about these things.

Now, these truths are in a sense themselves subordinate to even larger truths, truths concerning the existence of God, naturalism, humanity, and purpose. If we have reason to study the former, then a fortiori, we have reason to study and explore the latter. This is only sensible: the implications of whether or not God exists are vast, perhaps vaster than anything else. It matters for the purpose things may have, for the metaphysical nature of good and evil, for our anthropology, for our ideas about the afterlife, and so on. We thus have ample reason to seek evidence concerning the existence of God and, if God exists, to seek God himself.

Of course, not everybody is well-equipped to study complicated arguments for and against God's existence. Not everyone on earth has easy access to the thoughts and arguments of atheists – take the current population of Iran, for instance. And not everybody on earth has good access to the thoughts and arguments of religious believers – think of the increasing numbers of highly secular bubbles (even though, undoubtedly, access will be somewhat easier there). A plausible way to think of this situation, then, is that how much reason people have to delve into this is highly person dependent. For instance, it depends on their personal circumstances, whom they happen to know and whom they have access to, and how much education and intellectual formation they've had. We should expect different things from a highly educated philosophy professor in São Paulo than from an illiterate farmer in northern Mongolia.

The Great Pumpkin and the Religions of the World

If there's good reason to seek evidence concerning God's existence or nonexistence, is there also reason to find out whether other, perhaps crazier things exist? Maybe there's a Great Pumpkin, or perhaps our civilization was founded by Martians. If we fail to believe in them, aren't we missing out on some really important truths as well? In other words, are there any principled limits to this inquiry? And if not, why start this endless quest in the first place?

Fortunately, I think there are some principled limits here. The status of belief in God is simply rather different from that of belief in, say, Martians, the Great Pumpkin, unicorns, and leprechauns. Belief in God is shared by billions of normal, healthy, rational individuals, it has been the object of rigorous theological and philosophical scrutiny, and it has inspired millions to the greatest achievements in the arts and sciences. It would be unwise – to put it mildly – to take an a priori highly implausible theory about Martians or a Great Pumpkin as seriously as belief in God.

What about the thousands of world religions and life orientations? Should we all delve not only into atheism, Christianity, Islam, Judaism, Hinduism, and Buddhism, in their countless varieties, but also into Yazdânism? Should we study Zoroastrianism, such as the movement of Behāfarīd, Mazdakism, and Zurvanism? Should we explore hundreds, if not thousands, of religions and spiritual traditions that most of us have never heard of? In all fairness, wouldn't that just be infeasible?

To be sure, that would be too demanding. But let's not forget that religions can agree on many important things; for instance, that there is a God, that humans have been created, that there is an afterlife, or that there is meaning to human life on earth. Religions are fully compatible on many issues, so one doesn't need to explore all religions to rule out all the others. Moreover, if polytheism in general faces certain problems, one doesn't have to study the thousands of varieties of polytheism. To the extent that they are polytheistic, they face the same worries. Perhaps the best way to think of this, then, is that we all have good reason to explore at least the main worldviews, such as belief in God and atheism. Once one opts for, say, monotheism, one will have to consider the main possibilities there. And so on, keeping in mind that, no matter what worldview or religion one ends up choosing, various elements of that worldview or religion are compatible with many others.

The Paradoxical Nature of Faith

So far, we've confined ourselves almost entirely to belief. We saw that we can't choose what we believe, but that an honest and open-minded search for truth will inevitably influence what we believe and what we don't believe. Yet, our choice of life orientation depends not just on the evidence we stumble upon but equally on what we are willing to commit ourselves to. And this has everything to do with the nature of faith. Let me explain.

Faith used to be conceptualized in terms of propositional belief. The idea was that you have faith in God only if you believe certain things about God, such as that God exists and that he is perfectly good. However, this approach has been problematized over the last few decades. Lately, faith has been understood more often in terms of trust, hope, allegiance, and similar attitudes.[10] The Old Testament figure of Abraham, one of the Hebrew patriarchs, is often called the father of faith. But we know very little about what

---

[10] See, among others, the writings of Jonathan Kvanvig, "Affective Theism and People of Faith," *Midwest Studies in Philosophy* 37, no. 1 (2013): 109–128; *Faith and Humility* (Oxford: Oxford University Press, 2018); Daniel J. McKaughan, "Authentic Faith and Acknowledged Risk: Dissolving the Problem of Faith and Reason," *Religious Studies* 49, no. 1 (2013): 101–124; Daniel Howard-Snyder, "Propositional Faith: What It Is and What It Is Not," *American Philosophical Quarterly* 50, no. 4 (2013): 357–372; Meghan Page, "The Posture of Faith," *Oxford Studies in Philosophy of Religion* 8 (2017): 227–244.

exactly he believed. We do know, though, that he often trusted God and the promises God had made to him. Apparently, having faith is a matter of trusting God, committing yourself, or hoping, rather than believing a list of propositions. I think this is important, for it means that you can have faith in God even if you have doubts about God's existence – in fact, even if your doubts are so strong that you don't have the full-fledged belief that God exists. Another reason why this matters is that whether or not we believe in God also involves our will. We already saw that Thomas Nagel wouldn't want God to exist even if he had plenty of evidence for God. This is something I love about faith: it has everything to do with an open-minded search for truth, but it leaves plenty of room for our own choices and, thus, our own responsibility.

For religious believers, things may be even more complicated here. For a widely influential religious idea is that faith is also a gift from God. This idea is expressed in various Bible passages, such as Ephesians 2:8–10:

> For it is by grace you have been saved, through faith – and this is not from yourselves, it is the gift of God – not by works, so that no one can boast. For we are God's handiwork, created in Christ Jesus to do good works, which God prepared in advance for us to do.

Or take the *Catechism of the Catholic Church* on the nature of faith:

> When St. Peter confessed that Jesus is the Christ, the Son of the living God, Jesus declared to him that this revelation did not come "from flesh and blood," but from "my Father who is in heaven." *Faith is a gift of God, a supernatural virtue infused by him.* "Before this faith can be exercised, man must have the grace of God to move and assist him; he must have the interior helps of the Holy Spirit, who moves the heart and converts it to God, who opens the eyes of the mind and 'makes it easy for all to accept and believe the truth.'"[11]

[11] See, for instance, www.catholic-catechism.com/ccc_153.424.440.442.552.553.586.849.8 81.1444.htm.

188

Man can acquire religious faith, then, only by the grace of God. And I guess the same is meant to apply to women and people who identify neither as men nor as women. Despite one or two disagreements on a couple of other issues, the Reformation very much agrees with the Catholic tradition on the nature of faith as a gift. Says Luther:

> The second type of first birth is faith which we attribute to God. It is the chief constituent of the whole Christian nature. Faith puts to death the old man. It makes new children which henceforth bring thoughts and goals in accordance with God's. This first birth is God's blessing and His own work. No one should take it upon himself, that is no one should understand faith as coming out of his own powers as many do. When they hear of faith they consider it as something they receive by an act of their own will. In this way they credit themselves with what alone belongs to God since it is purely a divine work to have true faith.[12]

Now, God, if he exists, clearly doesn't give faith to everyone. Or at least not that we know. Some people report that they've honestly sought him and yet did not find him.[13] God remains hidden to them. Searching for God, then, is no guarantee for finding God or for becoming a person of religious faith. Again, thinking about these things reveals how complex and paradoxical the notion of faith is: it has to do with open-mindedly searching for the truth about reality, it involves our will, and yet it's also a gift. Anyone who abandons atheism and starts to explore religious faith will stumble upon new

---

[12] See Martin Luther, *The Festival Sermons of Martin Luther* (Michigan: Mark V Publications, 2005), 238.

[13] As we saw in chapter 6, the problem of divine hiddenness has been dealt with extensively in the work of John Schellenberg. See particularly his "Divine Hiddenness Justifies Atheism," in *Contemporary Debates in Philosophy of Religion*, ed. Michael L. Peterson and Raymond J. VanArragon (Oxford: Blackwell, 2004), 30–41; *Prolegomena to a Philosophy of Religion* (Ithaca: Cornell University Press, 2005); "Why Am I a Nonbeliever? – I Wonder …," in *50 Voices of Disbelief: Why We Are Atheists*, ed. Russell Blackford and Udo Schüklenk (Oxford: Wiley-Blackwell, 2009), 28–32.

intellectual challenges, and it's up for debate whether they can be met. But this book is about atheism, so I leave that for another occasion.[14]

The Adventure of Seeking the Truth about God

We saw that there are good pragmatic, moral, and intellectual reasons to explore the existence, nature, and character of God, to study atheism and its rivals. From what I said, it might seem as if pragmatic, moral, and intellectual reasons always neatly come apart. Yet, they are clearly narrowly interwoven. I've myself often experienced incredible joy, delight, and excitement in exploring what may well be the very foundations of reality: the nature of the cosmos, the existence of God, necessity and contingency, the miracle of life, and the beauty of the world. And I know of countless others with similar experiences. Naturally, all this also comes with the unsettling experience of thinking through evil, suffering, loneliness and despair, and plain ugliness. Yet, studying these phenomena comes with the strangely consoling feeling that one is addressing things of tremendous importance. As we saw, humans aren't the only beings of value in the universe; we may not even be the most important things to exist. Still, in this vast cosmos, with its unparalleled quantities of matter, and on our planet, where we are surrounded by other forms of life, for all we know we are the only ones actually able to gaze both inward and outward and ask the question of why we are here. There is a certain deep satisfaction in time and again returning to the big questions of life and getting a better grip on what can be known and coming to better see what we don't yet know, and maybe never will. I believe every one of us can only benefit from embarking on this great adventure.

---

[14] A core question here is how these three things go together in faith: honestly seeking evidence, voluntarily committing oneself to God, and faith's being a gift. I believe the notion of influence can play an important role here; see my "God, Evidence, and the Duty to Inquire," in *Belief and the Will*, ed. Nicolas Faucher, The New Synthese Historical Library (Dordrecht: Springer, forthcoming).

Selected Bibliography

Alexander, Scott. "New Atheism: The Godlessness That Failed." *Slate Star Codex* (blog), October 30, 2019. https://slatestarcodex.com/2019/10/30/new-atheism-the-godlessness-that-failed/.

Ali, Ayaan Hirsi. *Infidel*. New York: Free Press, 2007.

Alston, William P. *Perceiving God: The Epistemology of Religious Experience*. Ithaca: Cornell University Press, 1991.

Antony, Louise M., ed. *Philosophers without Gods: Meditations on Atheism and the Secular Life*. Oxford: Oxford University Press, 2007.

Baggini, Julian. *Atheism: A Very Short Introduction*. Oxford: Oxford University Press, 2003.

Bering, Jesse. *The God Instinct: The Psychology of Souls, Destiny, and the Meaning of Life*. London: Nicholas Brealey, 2011.

Blackford, Russell, and Udo Schüklenk, eds. *50 Voices of Disbelief: Why We Are Atheists*. Oxford: Wiley-Blackwell, 2009.

Boudry, Maarten, and Massimo Pigliucci, eds. *Science Unlimited? The Challenges of Scientism*. Chicago: University of Chicago Press, 2018.

Bullivant, Stephen, and Michael Ruse, eds. *The Oxford Handbook of Atheism*. Oxford: Oxford University Press, 2013.

Cliteur, Paul. "The Definition of Atheism." *Journal of Religion and Society* 11 (2009): 1–23.

Collins, Francis S. *The Language of God: A Scientist Presents Evidence for Belief*. New York: Free Press, 2006.

Craig, William Lane, and J. P. Moreland, eds. *The Blackwell Companion to Natural Theology*. Oxford: Wiley-Blackwell, 2012.

Dawkins, Richard. *A Devil's Chaplain: Reflections on Hope, Lies, Science, and Love*. Boston: Houghton Mifflin, 2004.

Dawkins, Richard. *The God Delusion*. London: Bantam, 2006.

Dawkins, Richard. *Outgrowing God: A Beginner's Guide*. London: Bantam, 2019.

Dawkins, Richard. *The Selfish Gene.* 2nd ed. Oxford: Oxford University Press, 1989. First published 1976.

De Botton, Alain. *Religion for Atheists: A Non-believer's Guide to the Uses of Religion.* London: Hamish Hamilton, 2012.

De Ridder, Jeroen. "Science and Scientism in Popular Science Writing." *Social Epistemology Review and Reply Collective* 3, no. 12 (2014): 23–39.

De Ridder, Jeroen, Rik Peels, and René van Woudenberg, eds. *Scientism: Prospects and Problems.* New York: Oxford University Press, 2018.

Dennett, Daniel C. *Breaking the Spell: Religion as a Natural Phenomenon.* New York: Penguin Group, 2006.

Ecklund, Elaine Howard, and David R. Johnson. *Varieties of Atheism in Science.* New York: Oxford University Press, 2021.

Everitt, Nicholas. *The Non-existence of God.* London: Routledge, 2004.

Flew, Antony. *The Presumption of Atheism and Other Philosophical Essays on God, Freedom and Immortality.* London: Elek/Pemberton, 1976.

Gray, John. *Seven Types of Atheism.* London: Penguin Books, 2018.

Grayling, A. C. *The God Argument: The Case against Religion and for Humanism.* London: Bloomsbury, 2013.

Harris, Sam. *Letter to a Christian Nation.* London: Bantam, 2007.

Harrison, Peter. *The Bible, Protestantism, and the Rise of Natural Science.* Cambridge: Cambridge University Press, 1998.

Harrison, Peter. *The Fall of Man and the Foundations of Science.* Cambridge: Cambridge University Press, 2007.

Harrison, Peter, and Jon Roberts. *Science without God? Rethinking the History of Scientific Naturalism.* Oxford: Oxford University Press, 2019.

Hitchens, Christopher. *Letters to a Young Contrarian.* New York: Basic Books, 2001.

Hitchens, Christopher, ed. *The Portable Atheist: Essential Readings for the Nonbeliever.* Cambridge, MA: Da Capo, 2007.

Hitchens, Christopher, Richard Dawkins, Sam Harris, and Daniel Dennett. *The Four Horsemen: The Conversation That Sparked an Atheist Revolution.* New York: Random House, 2019.

Howard-Snyder, Daniel. "The Evolutionary Argument for Atheism." In *Being, Freedom, and Method: Themes from the Philosophy of Peter van Inwagen,* edited by John A. Keller, 241–262. Oxford: Oxford University Press, 2017.

Howard-Snyder, Daniel, and Paul K. Moser, eds. *Divine Hiddenness: New Essays*. Cambridge: Cambridge University Press, 2002.

Kvanvig, Jonathan. *Faith and Humility*. Oxford: Oxford University Press, 2018.

Lennox, John. *Gunning for God: A Critique of the New Atheism*. Oxford: Lion, 2011.

Lovering, Rob. *God and Evidence: Problems for Theistic Philosophers*. New York: Bloomsbury, 2018.

Mackie, John L. *The Miracle of Theism: Arguments for and against the Existence of God*. Oxford: Clarendon, 1982.

Marsden, George. *The Soul of the American Academy: From Protestant Establishment to Established Nonbelief*. New York: Oxford University Press, 1994.

Martin, Michael. *Atheism: A Philosophical Justification*. Philadelphia: Temple University Press, 1990.

Marty, Martin E., and R. Scott Appleby, eds. *The Fundamentalism Project*. 5 vols. Chicago: University of Chicago Press, 1991–1995.

Mawson, Tim J. "The Ethics of Believing in God." *Think* 9, no. 25 (2010): 93–100.

McGrath, Alister. *The Twilight of Atheism: The Rise and Fall of Disbelief in the Modern World*. London: Rider, 2004.

Metaxas, Eric. *Is Atheism Dead?* Washington, DC: Salem Books, 2021.

Nagel, Thomas. *The Last Word*. New York: Oxford University Press, 1997.

Paas, Stefan, and Rik Peels. *God bewijzen: Argumenten voor en tegen geloven*. Amsterdam: Balans, 2013.

Peels, Rik. "Does Evolution Conflict with God's Character?" *Modern Theology* 34, no. 4 (2018): 544–564.

Peels, Rik. "God, Evidence, and the Duty to Inquire." In *Belief and the Will*, edited by Nicolas Faucher. The New Synthese Historical Library. Dordrecht: Springer, forthcoming.

Peels, Rik. "Is Omniscience Impossible?" *Religious Studies* 49, no. 4 (2013): 481–490.

Peels, Rik. *Responsible Belief: A Theory in Ethics and Epistemology*. New York: Oxford University Press, 2017.

Peels, Rik. "Scientism and Scientific Fundamentalism: What Science Can Learn from Mainstream Religion." *Interdisciplinary Science Reviews* (2022). https://doi.org/10.1080/03080188.2022.2152246.

Philipse, Herman. *God in the Age of Science? A Critique of Religious Reason.* Oxford: Oxford University Press, 2012.

Philipse, Herman. *Reason and Religion: Evaluating and Explaining Belief in Gods.* Cambridge: Cambridge University Press, 2022.

Plantinga, Alvin. *Warranted Christian Belief.* New York: Oxford University Press, 2000.

Plantinga, Alvin, and Nicholas Wolterstorff, eds. *Faith and Rationality: Reason and Belief in God.* Notre Dame: University of Notre Dame Press, 1983.

Rosenberg, Alex. *The Atheist's Guide to Reality: Enjoying Life without Illusions.* New York: W. W. Norton, 2011.

Russell, Bertrand. *Why I Am Not a Christian.* London: Routledge, 1996.

Ruthven, Malise. *Fundamentalism: The Search for Meaning.* Oxford: Oxford University Press, 2004.

Savater, Fernando. *La vida eterna.* Madrid: Mateu Cromo, 2007.

Shermer, Michael. *How We Believe: Science, Skepticism, and the Search for God.* New York: Henry Holt, 2003.

Stenmark, Mikael. *Scientism: Science, Ethics and Religion.* New York: Routledge, 2018.

Stump, Eleonore. *Wandering in Darkness: Narrative and the Problem of Suffering.* Oxford: Oxford University Press, 2010.

Swinburne, Richard. *The Existence of God.* 2nd ed. Oxford: Clarendon, 2004.

Van Woudenberg, René. "Truths That Science Cannot Touch." *Philosophia Reformata* 76, no. 2 (2011): 169–186.

Visser, Harm, ed. *Leven zonder God: Elf interviews over ongeloof.* Amsterdam/Antwerp: L. J. Veen, 2003.

Vitz, Paul C. *Faith of the Fatherless: The Psychology of Atheism.* Dallas: Spence, 1999.

Wilson, David Sloan. *Darwin's Cathedral: Evolution, Religion, and the Nature of Society.* Chicago: University of Chicago Press, 2002.

Wolpert, Lewis. *The Unnatural Nature of Science.* Cambridge, MA: Harvard University Press, 1992.

Index

a se, God as being, 151
Abraham, 37, 41, 187
academia, 9, 58, 61, 135–143
ad hocness, 169–171
adventure, 21–23, 47, 173, 190
aesthetics, 48, 155
agnosticism, 5–6, 48, 149, 175–177, 180, 183
Alexander, Scott, 10–11
Ali, Ayaan Hirsi, 23–24, 30
allegiance, 187
Alpha Centurion, 111–112
Alston, William, 25, 52, 90, 178
anthropology, 56, 83, 167, 185
Antony, Louise, 21–22, 109
apatheism, 9
apologetics, 139
a priori objection against belief in
    God, 115
argument
    atheistic, 117–173
    from consciousness, 14, 90, 95
    cosmological, 14, 90, 95, 175
    from divine hiddenness, 102,
        165–169, 174
    epistemic, 118–20
    from fine-tuning, 14, 90, 95, 134, 172, 175
    God-of-the-gaps, 130–135
    from inefficiency, 145–147
    from miracles, 14, 175
    moral, 14, 90, 95, 118–120, 172, 175
    ontological, 14, 175
    from scale, 152–157
    theistic, 4, 134
Astarte, 106
asymmetry between religious belief and
    atheism, 98–99, 112–114

atheism
    arguments for, 11, 17, 20, 101, 110,
        117–174
    based on testimony, 109–111
    motivations for, 17–49, 91
    negative, 7
    positive, 5, 7, 13
    practical, 6
    presumption of, 89–91, 99, 102,
        115, 174
atheos, 105
Atkins, Peter, 61, 72
Augustine, 27, 29, 104, 122–123
autism, 48–49

Baal, 104, 106
Bach, Johann Sebastian, 102, 162
Baker-Hytch, Max, 32
belief
    basic, 91, 97, 107, 109, 115, 125
    by fiat, 178
    commonsense, 18, 66, 73–75, 87, 88
    control of, 180
    influence on, 178–180, 182–183, 187
    memory, 74, 87, 92, 94, 97
    metaphysical, 74, 87
    moral, 66–68
    nonbasic, 91
    properly basic, 91–92, 94–97, 104
    religious, 4, 33, 67, 98, 100, 111, 136, 138,
        139, 160, 170
Bering, Jesse, 67, 98
Bible, 9, 36, 39, 42, 126–129, 155–156, 161,
    164, 168, 188
bigfoot, 100, 112–113
biodiversity, 62, 147, 184

BioLogos Institute, 133–134
biology, 27, 56, 59–60, 65, 79, 83, 146, 184–185
Blackford, Russell, 110
Bonhoeffer, Dietrich, 27, 29, 132–133
Boudry, Maarten, 16, 34
Boyle's law, 109, 110
brain system
  analytic, 138–139
  intuitive, 138–139
Bruno, Giordano, 156
Buddhism, 8, 186

Calvin, John, 90, 94, 154–155
caricature, 35–38
Carroll, Sean, 152–153
Catechism of the Catholic Church, 188–189
causal connection between belief and world, 97–98
certainty, 76, 79, 81, 82, 84
choosing to believe, 53, 177–178, 182, 187
Christianity, 14, 27, 36, 43–47, 86, 102, 129, 147, 154–157, 165, 170, 172
Clark, Thomas, 34, 57–58
Clifford, William, 33
cognitive framework, 50–51, 86–87
cognitive science of religion, 4, 68, 138–139
Collins, Francis, 27, 29, 134, 142
common sense, 18, 55, 57, 64–66, 76, 88
  knowledge from, 75, 84
  science as based on, 73–75
condition
  necessary, 78, 80, 123
  sufficient, 80
consciousness, 19, 82, 126, 132, 150, 176, 183
contingency, 112, 151, 190
Copernicus, Nicolaus, 27, 156
cosmic fine-tuning, 126, 132
cosmos, 65, 100–102, 129, 154, 156, 171, 190
Coulson, Charles, 133
counterintuitiveness, 64–66
COVID-19, 63, 91, 92, 129, 178
Craig, William Lane, 1, 25
creation, 93, 146, 151, 153–157
  humans as the jewel of, 153–154
creationism, 129–131, 147

Crick, Francis, 59–60
Crusade, 40

Darwin, Charles, 6, 59, 151, 159, 160
Darwinism, 159–160, 162–163
Dawkins, Richard, 3, 12, 23, 41–42, 50–51, 59, 83, 104, 125–128, 131, 145–148
de Botton, Alain, 119–120
de facto, 103
de re, 103
de Ridder, Jeroen, 58, 71, 107
debunking argument, 13, 57, 66–70
defeater, 92–95, 112, 113
  rebutting, 70, 92
  undercutting, 70, 92–93
Dennett, Daniel, 3, 13, 50, 60, 151, 158–159
design, 1, 56, 57, 111, 145–146, 151, 160
determinism, 86
disagreement, 63–64
distantionism, 52–55, 86
divine hiddenness, 102, 116, 165–170, 173, 189
doctrine, 3, 4, 8, 11, 83, 105
dogmatism, 24, 33, 82, 106
Dostoyevsky, Fyodor, 27, 88, 158
  The Brothers Karamazov, 158
doxastic involuntarism, 178
Draper, Paul, 100, 159–160
Drummond, Henry, 130
dualism, 79–80, 82
Dupré, John, 88

Ecklund, Elaine Howard, 136
education, 137, 139–141, 185
efficiency, 145–148
Endō, Shūsaku, 88
epistemology, 25, 91–93, 103, 113
Europe, 26, 91, 136, 137, 140
Everitt, Nicholas, 19–20, 153, 155
evidence, 28, 33, 37, 38, 46, 87, 92, 114–115, 148, 176, 178, 179, 188
  against God's existence, 163
  for atheism, 6, 174
  of design, 160
  for the existence of exotic beings, 113
  in favor of Christianity, 14

for God's existence, 1, 14, 53, 54, 133,
167, 175, 183
nonargumentative, 54
from personal suffering, 32
evidentialism, 51–52, 86
evolutionary explanation, 68, 69, 184
evolutionary theory, 37, 61, 62, 77, 83, 86,
146, 185
ex nihilo, 132
experience
lack of, 116
mystical, 93, 103, 134, 176
experiment, scientific, 69–70, 121–122, 124
extraterrestrial life, 115
extremism, 82, 83

fairies, 112
faith
as a gift, 189
maturity of, 117, 124, 134
nature of, 38, 190
religious, 36–37, 106, 118, 122, 127, 130,
143–144, 174, 189
family resemblance, 78–81
fanaticism, 83
Farias, Miguel, 24
father issues, 49
Flew, Antony, 25, 89, 113
flounder, 145
folk stupidity, 82
free will, 56, 57, 60, 69–70, 82, 87, 162–63
fundamentalism, 35, 76–80, 83, 117
Christian, 12, 147
scientific, 80–83
fundamentals, 77

Galilei, Galileo, 27, 156
Garber, Daniel, 53
geocentricism, 157
Gervais, Will, 138
ghosts, 139
God
absence of, 100–107
as creator, 7, 106, 122, 124, 145–151
efficiency of, 145–148
existence of, 3, 45, 63, 102–103, 108, 112,
115, 124, 185, 190

faith in, 18, 143–144, 117, 118, 120, 144,
187–190
of the gaps, 130–135
intentions of, 129, 146–148, 150, 155, 156,
164, 165, 171–172
knowledge of, 75, 84, 89–90, 123
presence of, 46, 103, 109, 133, 167
relationship with, 51, 143, 166–168,
173, 183
as a spirit, 101, 109
of the weak, 43–44, 160–161
Gray, Asa, 27, 160
Gray, John, 3, 5, 35, 125
Grayling, A. C., 4, 105, 170
Great Pumpkin, 112, 186

hagiography, 29
hamartiology, 11
Harris, John, 114
Harris, Sam, 3, 7, 11, 13, 50, 60, 89, 113, 128,
130, 145–147
Harrison, Peter, 26, 129
harshness of life, 100–101
heliocentrism, 156
henotheism, 106
hero, 27–30
Higgs boson, 62
Hinduism, 18, 78, 85, 107, 186
hinge proposition, 18–19
Hinn, Benny, 164
Hitchens, Christopher, 3, 15, 40, 50,
118–119
Hobrink, Ben, 129
Holland, Aaron, 89, 113
hope, 20, 22, 37, 47, 80, 84, 123, 165, 187
Human Genome Project, 29, 142
humanities, 55, 56, 75–76, 88, 171
Hume, David, 151, 158
Huxley, Thomas, 6
Hyperactive Agency Detection Device
(HADD), 67, 98
hypothesis, 51, 54, 124–126, 143, 153

Ichneumonidae, 160
illusion, 1, 23, 28, 70, 82, 85, 183
image of God, 49, 106, 117, 124, 160–165,
169, 172–173

imago Dei, 26, 85, 154
imperialism, scientific, 88
incomprehensibility of God, 171, 180
independence, intellectual, 21–27
induction, 96
infallibility
  of holy scriptures, 79, 84
  of science, 84
infinity, 103–104, 181
intellectual authority, 21, 22
intelligence, 22, 137, 142, 151
  analytic, 137–139
  creative, 138
  cultural, 138
  emotional, 138
  practical, 138
  social, 138
intelligent design, 81, 131–132, 146
introspection, 60, 74, 94, 96–97
intuition, 18, 75, 95, 101, 116, 125, 127, 138
  metaphysical, 87
  moral, 37, 42, 55, 88
irrationality, 64, 95, 112, 118, 119, 174
Islam, 7, 9, 18, 20, 81, 84, 96, 101,
    106, 107, 112, 124, 127, 149, 174,
    184, 186

Jephthah, 41–42
Jesus Christ, 17, 39, 43–44, 46, 51, 128, 143,
    161, 171, 188
Job, 43, 161, 164–165
Judaism, 7, 18, 43, 78, 85, 86, 96, 101, 106,
    112, 124, 127, 149, 184, 186

kalam cosmological argument, 172
Keysar, Ariela, 13
Küng, Hans, 157

laboratory, 122
Laden, Anthony Simon, 22–23
Ladyman, James, 60
Lamentations, 43, 161
Libet, Benjamin, 69–70
life, existence of, 152–153
literalism, 36, 79, 84, 127, 154
liturgy, 52, 54, 55, 134, 162, 180
logical positivism, 25, 72, 120

Louis, Ard, viii
Luther, Martin, 24, 189

MacIntyre, Alasdair, 25
Mackie, John L., 51–52, 89, 114
macrolevel, 65, 66
Malick, Terrence, 163
  The Tree of Life, 163
Manicheism, 79, 82
Marsden, George, 77
Martin, Michael, 89, 113
mass, 54, 182
material object, 66, 85, 124, 150
materialism, 86
matter, uselessness of, 152–153
memory, 65, 73, 96, 179
mesolevel, 65–66
Metaxas, Eric, 14, 29
microlevel, 65, 66
Midgley, Mary, 73
miracle, 58, 67, 126, 171
Mizrahi, Moti, 75–76
modernity, 77, 79, 81–82
morality, 21, 28, 36, 60, 61, 82, 87, 126–127,
    177, 183
Mother Teresa, 169

Nagel, Thomas, 20, 188
narrative, 13–14, 43, 45, 76, 79–80, 82
naturalism, 4, 34, 86, 97, 126, 185
Navarro-Rivera, Juhem, 13
neuroscience, 60, 84
New Atheism, 3–4, 11–13, 125, 148, 158
Nietzsche, Friedrich, 10, 28, 165–166
Norenzaya, Ara, 138
North America, 26, 140
Nouwen, Henri, 44–45, 161

omnipresence, 108, 109
onus of proof, 89, 114
Orthodox Church, 86

Paas, Stefan, 135
Pascal, Blaise, 27, 29, 53
  wager of, 53–54, 180–183
Paul, 25
Peels-de Waal, Marjolijn, ix

peer pressure, 48, 141
perception, 65, 73, 94, 103
  fact, 1
  object, 1
perfect-being theology, 168, 172
person, 66
  of faith, 84, 142–144, 180, 189
  God as a, 150, 168, 172
  supernatural, 7
Philipse, Herman, 16, 104, 105, 171
philosophy of religion, 14, 25, 89, 139, 175
philosophy of science, 120
physicalism, 86–87
Pigliucci, Massimo, 34, 60
plaice, 145
Plantinga, Alvin, 25, 29, 52, 90, 94
polytheism, 85, 105, 106, 186
poor, 43–45, 161, 162
possession, 43–45, 53, 182
prayer, 2, 18, 52, 67, 93, 141, 143, 165,
    170, 180
  efficacy of, 120–124
  intercessory, 120–122
Proba, 122
problem of divine hiddenness, 94,
    165–169, 189
problem of evil, 94, 157–165
Protestantism, 24, 86
Provine, William, 56–57

Quine, W. V. O., 96
Qur'an, 39, 79, 84

racism, 11, 12
Rea, Michael, 168
reactionary movement, 79, 81
reasons to seek God
  intellectual, 184–186
  moral, 183–184
  pragmatic, 180–183
reductio ad absurdum, 112
reductionism, 61, 84, 86
Reformation, 189
Reformed epistemology, 52, 89–90,
    93–94
relationship, 46–47, 51, 119, 143, 166–168,
    173, 183

religion, Abrahamic, 7, 37, 120
repugnance
  aesthetic, 48
  moral, 38–43
revelation, 7, 75, 83, 85, 127–130, 134, 188
ritual, 53, 54, 80, 119, 120, 180
Roman Catholicism, 24, 40, 85, 86
Rosenberg, Alex, 28–29, 61, 62, 65, 135
Russell, Bertrand, 28, 37, 39–40, 148
Russell's teapot, 148–150
Russia, 178

Sagan, Carl, 13, 82
Schellenberg, John, 20, 166, 189
Schlick, Moritz, 72, 120
Schüklenk, Udo, 110
science, 62–70, 73–76, 83–86
  application of, 63
  foundation of, 73–75, 88
  principles of, 74–75
  success of, 62–63, 82
scientism, 55–59, 61–62, 68, 70–73, 75–77,
    80–82, 87
  bold, 60–61, 70, 73, 75
  fundamental argument against, 73–75
  modest, 59–60, 68, 70, 75, 87
Scriven, Michael, 89, 113
Second World War, 29
secularity, 140–141
self-referential incoherence, 70–72
sensus divinitatis, 52, 94, 103, 104
sexism, 11, 12
Shapiro, Steward, 30–31
Shermer, Michael, 14, 34, 131–132, 152
Simpson, G. G., 59
skepticism, 33–35, 168
  science, 81, 82
Smart, J. J. C., 58
Smart, Ninian, 77
social justice, 11, 12
Socrates, 72
soteriology, 11, 167
species, 57, 145–147
spirit, 139
status, 43–45, 163
Stenmark, Mikael, 10, 71
STEP, 121–122, 124

Street, Sharon, 67
Stump, Eleonore, 25, 32
suffering, 17, 30–32, 43, 47, 90, 100–101,
    146, 157–165, 167, 176, 190
supernatural power, 139
suspension of judgment, 5, 115, 175–177
Swaab, Dick, 60
Swinburne, Richard, 25, 27, 94–95
systematic theology, 109, 139, 171

terrorism, 82, 83
testimony, 18, 26, 109–111, 134, 175
theism, 20, 38, 51, 66
    as a hypothesis, 125
    meaninglessness of, 120
    negative, 5
    presumption of, 99, 113–116
Thomas Aquinas, 29, 90, 94, 123
Tillich, Paul, 149
Tooley, Michael, 89, 113
tradition, 4, 27, 29, 36, 38, 43, 68, 82, 84,
    106, 123, 127, 132, 134, 149, 180, 186, 189
trauma, 30–33, 136
troll, 112
trust, 33, 42, 45, 47, 63, 84, 110, 111, 138, 143,
    173, 187–188
truth, 2–3, 24, 33, 57, 58, 62, 63, 98,
    107, 118, 148, 166, 176–177, 184–185,
    187, 189
    a priori, 71
    analytic, 72
    moral, 67, 68, 116, 172
    scientific, 83, 129

uncertainty, 79, 81–84
unicorn, 112, 186
universe
    age of, 151, 152
    size of, 152, 153
unreasonableness, 118

Van Eyghen, Hans, 68
van Inwagen, Peter, 25
van Woudenberg, René, 73–74, 107
verification criterion, 72
Vermeer, Johannes, 54
vestigia Dei, 104
vice, 33
    intellectual, 33–35, 179
virtue, 33, 123
    intellectual, 33, 179
    supernatural, 188
von Bingen, Hildegard, 162

witch, 40
Wittgenstein, Ludwig, 18–19, 78–79, 120
Wolpert, Lewis, 1–3, 64–65
Wolterstorff, Nicholas, 25, 52, 55, 90
Woolf, Virginia, 88
worldview, 4, 7, 8, 32, 135, 140–141, 150,
    170, 187

yeti, 1, 112

Zagzebski, Linda, 33
Zeus, 7, 8, 104, 106
Zuckerman, Miron, 137, 142

Ingram Content Group UK Ltd.
Milton Keynes UK
UKHW010753250623
423921UK00014B/194

9 781009 297776